easy world craft

Paper Crafts

easy world craft

Paper Crafts

A handy step-by-step guide

DK

LONDON, NEW YORK, MELBOURNE,
MUNICH, DELHI

Project Editor Katharine Goddard
Senior Art Editors Glenda Fisher, Elaine Hewson
Managing Editor Penny Smith
Senior Managing Art Editor Marianne Markham
Jacket Creative Nicola Powling
Pre-Production Producer Rebecca Fallowfield
Creative Technical Support Sonia Charbonnier
Art Director Jane Bull
Publisher Mary Ling
Special Sales Creative Project Manager Alison Donovan

DK INDIA
Managing Editor Alicia Ingty
Editors Janashree Singha, Manasvi Vohra
Senior Art Editor Balwant Singh
Art Editor Vandna Sonkariya
Assistant Art Editor Nikita Sodhi
Managing Art Editor Navidita Thapa
Pre-Production Manager Sunil Sharma
DTP Designer Satish Chandra Gaur, Rajdeep Singh

First published in Great Britain in 2014
by Dorling Kindersley Limited
80 Strand, London WC2R 0RL

Material in this publication was previously published in:
Ultimate Christmas Book (2007),
The Christmas Book (2008),
Craft (2012), The Girls' Book of Crafts & Activities (2013)

A Penguin Random House Company

Copyright © 2007, 2008, 2012, 2013, 2014
Dorling Kindersley Limited

2 4 6 8 10 9 7 5 3 1

001 – 193356 – Mar/2014

A CIP catalogue record for this book is available
from the British Library

ISBN 978-1-4093-5438-3

Printed and bound in China by Hung Hing
Printing Co. Ltd.

Discover more at **www.dk.com/crafts**

Contents

Introduction

PAPERMAKING • PAPER MARBLING • PAPIER-MÂCHÉ • SCRAPBOOKING • LINO PRINTING

PAPER DECORATIONS • DÉCOUPAGE • PAPER PUNCHING • QUILLING

CARD-MAKING • BOX-MAKING • SCREEN PRINTING

Paper is such a familiar and humble material, it's easy to overlook how versatile it can be when it comes to crafting. In this book, you'll learn ways to transform paper into stationery, gifts, and decorative items. Because much of the paper used in these projects is recycled, the cost is minimal but the results are sensational.

Paper is an intrinsic part of our everyday lives. There are newspapers, magazines, catalogues, brochures, letters that are delivered to our door, brown paper parcels, cardboard cartons, and shoe boxes with their accompanying layers of tissue paper.

Paper accounts for about a third of municipal waste; at best it is recycled by pulping but at worst it is consigned to landfill. Once you've leafed through these pages and can see for yourself what can be done with a few pieces of paper and card, you'll view this modest and most basic of materials in a different light.

This book explains a wealth of paper-crafting techniques, as well as offering a number of inspiring and achievable projects, including a stationery set, postcards, homewares, and decorations.

With writing paper conjured up from paper pulp and petals or adorned with printed motifs, you can be at the forefront of a letter-writing revival. Instead of hoarding old photographs and letters in a drawer, use scrapbooking techniques to create an heirloom album. With a shoe box and a few scraps of giftwrap, you can make a keepsake box. And if there's something to celebrate, make your own greetings cards and gift boxes, or decorate a party venue with bold and colourful paper pompom decorations.

Paper might not be the first thing that comes to mind when you think of home accessories, so a punched lampshade or a quilled paper picture is likely to be something of a talking point. It's time to rescue all that paper from the recycling bin. Scissors at the ready? Get snipping and ripping!

Tools and Materials

Tools and materials

Scissors, sticky tape, paper, and glue are the kind of items you'll find in most households, so when tackling papercraft projects you won't need to make a large investment in specialist equipment. Try out the projects with the tools and materials you already have to hand before going out and buying any extra items.

Papermaking

Shredded waste paper
Use waste paper without too much dark printing, such as bank statements. Keep to one main colour if possible. Paper that has already been recycled, such as most newspaper, does not work so well as the fibres are too short.

Food colouring You can use powdered or liquid food colourings or even icing paste to correct the colour of homemade paper if the pulp looks a little drab.

Decorative additions Use dried flower petals and leaves; short scraps of colourful yarn, lace, or fabric; snippets of Angelina fibre; glitter; confetti; and sequins – almost anything small and flat – to add interest to homemade paper.

Mould and deckle A mould is a frame with netting stretched over it that holds the paper pulp. A deckle is the same size as the mould and sits on top of it. The deckle helps trap the pulp and shape the paper sheets. Both are available from craft shops, or you can make your own (see p.18).

Blender or food processor This makes mashing paper pulp effortless. You could use a potato masher instead, but it's hard work and takes a long time.

Absorbent cloths Use J cloths or old flannelette sheets cut a little larger than the mould to drain and dry homemade paper sheets. If the cloths are textured, your paper will be too.

Paper marbling

Good-quality paper
Use cartridge paper or watercolour paper for marbling. The paper need not be expensive but it does need to be sturdy enough to be handled when wet.

Acrylic or marbling paints
Acrylics work well but will probably need thinning with a little water; special marbling paints are better.

Cocktail sticks or twigs
Use these to drag the paint into swirls and patterns. The slimmer the stick, the more elegant the lines and swirls will be.

Wide-tooth comb Use an Afro comb or make an equivalent by taping halved cocktail sticks onto a 15cm (6in) ruler. This forms a comb-like tool that can be used to produce fan and feather patterns.

Fungicide-free wallpaper paste or marbling size
Mixed with water, this will form a jelly-like surface on which the marbling paints float.

Paintbrushes or pipettes Use these to distribute the paint. Pipettes work better when creating lines and large dots, but paintbrushes produce tiny dots and interesting splatters.

Papier-mâché

Recycled items Save packaging such as plastic containers, cardboard tubes, and plastic carrier bags, which can be combined to form basic shapes.

PVA glue Polyvinyl acetate adhesive, also known as white glue or woodworking adhesive, can be used straight from the container for glueing items together or it can be diluted to use as a paste for final layers.

Masking tape Use decorator's masking tape or sticky tape to join components when making a base for papier-mâché objects.

Newspapers Combine strips of old newspapers or pages from telephone directories and similar types of absorbent paper with wallpaper paste. This forms a paper pulp which, when dry, hardens to a tough shell.

Tissue paper Instead of painting designs on the surface of a papier-mâché object, you can use coloured tissue paper to form a final layer or to apply cutout shapes.

Wallpaper paste This is used to create the paper pulp and should be made by mixing with water, according to the instructions on the packet.

Scrapbooking

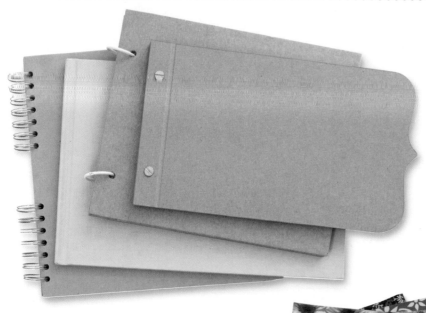

Ribbons and borders Ribbons can be used to attach labels, to tie into bows, or to create borders. Self-adhesive ribbons are also available.

Albums Modern scrapbooks are available in a variety of formats, with 30 x 30cm (12 x 12in) being the most popular. Some have pages bound in, while many albums are loose-leaf.

Printed and decorative papers Choose from a wide variety of patterned and plain papers, and papers with deckle edges to add interest to plain scrapbooking pages.

Deckle-edged scissors Use scissors with shaped blades to cut decorative edges on paper. Various shapes are available, from the familiar pinking (zigzag) blades, to scallops, wave shapes, and many others.

Card and paper Plain coloured card and paper are useful for creating backgrounds.

Charms and accents These little items – jewels, sequins, tiny frames, and other specially manufactured decorations – add the final flourish to scrapbooking pages.

Adhesives Various glues are used for different applications. A glue stick will stick papers and photographs, while glue dots are useful for applying small decorative elements.

Small envelopes These can be used for hidden journalling (see p.35) and they are also useful for storing small components ready for use in scrapbooking projects.

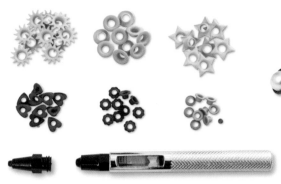

Eyelets and eyelet setter Eyelets are used to create neat holes in a page, which are useful for threading with ribbons and cords. An eyelet setting tool usually combines a hole punch and a tool for attaching the eyelet.

Brads Otherwise known as paper fasteners, these consist of a stud with two prongs on the back, which are inserted into a hole punched in paper. The prongs are then opened out and flattened, keeping the brad in place. Use them to hold components on a page or simply as decoration.

Page protectors For loose-leaf albums, you'll need plastic sleeves – also known as page protectors.

Rubber stamps Choose picture stamps for adding decorative touches, and alphabet and word stamps for captions and titles. Use an ink pad or brush pens to apply multiple colours to stamps.

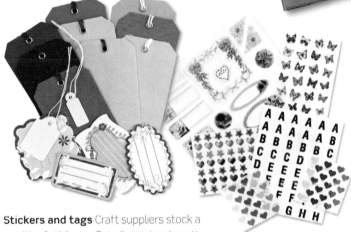

Stickers and tags Craft suppliers stock a wealth of stickers – flat, dimensional, matt, shiny, holographic, metallic, plush, and so on – to decorate scrapbooking pages, as well as labels and tags, all of which can be used in imaginative ways.

Lino printing

Lino cutting tools Buy a selection of three or four tools – including narrow, medium, and wide gouges – and a couple of safety handles.

Inks Specialist lino printing inks are available in a range of intermixable colours. Choose water-based inks as they do not contain solvents and are easy to clean off.

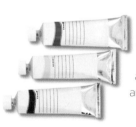

Carbon paper Use this with a hard pencil (such as an H or 2H) for transferring designs to the surface of the lino.

Lino This is available in pre-cut squares and rectangles, or buy a large piece and cut it yourself.

Roller Buy a roller in a width to suit the size of lino you are using.

Paper decorations

Découpage

Small scissors Choose small, sharp scissors with pointed blades for getting into corners and cutting out the tiniest areas of a design.

Paper Use printed papers that have a pattern of separate, distinct motifs that can easily be cut out. Many craft suppliers sell papers that have been specially designed for découpage.

Paper All kinds of paper can be used – you can recycle magazine pages for bunting and cardboard boxes for card cutouts – but tissue paper and crepe paper are particularly useful and come in a range of vivid, eye-catching colours.

Varnish The paper surface of the découpage needs to be sealed to protect it, so varnish is important. Choose a water-based varnish as it is solvent-free and you can wash the brush used to apply it with water.

Découpage medium This is the best choice of adhesive to stick down paper cutouts. It is easy to apply with a paintbrush and has a milky appearance so that you can visibly ensure an even coating. It allows the paper to be repositioned as needed and doesn't make the paper buckle.

Paper punching

Quilling

Lever punches These come in a range of sizes to punch a variety of shapes. Regular punches punch the shape close to the edge of the paper; long-arm punches reach further in.

Anywhere punches These come in two parts which align with the paper in between, using strong magnets. Shapes can be punched anywhere and at any angle on the paper.

Spring-loaded punches These punches are used to cut small holes for decoration or to insert brads or eyelets.

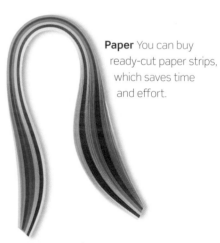

Paper You can buy ready-cut paper strips, which saves time and effort.

Eyelet/hole punch This hand-held punch is designed to be used with a small heavy hammer. Hold the tool upright with the paper on a punching mat and hit sharply with the hammer to cut a hole.

Paper There is a wide variety of paper in different weights and thicknesses. Choose a paper suitable for the project. Some papers are soft and difficult to punch through; others are crisp and punch cleanly.

Punching mat Small cutting mats are specially made to use with eyelet/hole punches. Ordinary cutting mats would be irreparably damaged if used to punch holes.

Quilling tools A quilling tool is a plastic stick with a slit in the top for inserting the end of a paper strip. Tools are often sold in sets, with slits of various sizes to accommodate papers of different widths.

Box-making

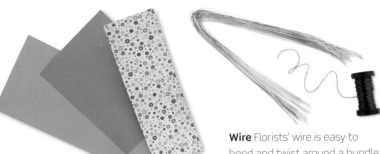

Card All kinds of card can be used to make boxes, including coloured and printed card. Make sure the card is thick enough to hold its shape.

Wire Florists' wire is easy to bend and twist around a bundle of paper to make flower or other paper decorations to go with your box. If you have garden wire, you could substitute this, or use paper-covered wire.

YOU WILL ALSO NEED...

Ruler Use a metal ruler for cutting; a plastic ruler is also useful for measuring and drawing straight lines.

Scissors These are an essential tool for cutting paper. Use a large, sturdy pair for cutting large sheets of paper and card; use smaller scissors for more detailed work.

Sticky tape This is useful for securing paper, for example, when wrapping a gift. Double-sided sticky tape can often be used instead of glue, for sticking down pieces of paper invisibly and securely.

Adhesives A glue stick is useful for paper, while an all-purpose glue forms a strong bond for attaching sequins, gems, and other small items to paper.

Cutting mat A self-healing cutting mat is essential when cutting card and paper using a metal ruler and craft knife. These mats are usually printed with a grid of straight lines so they are also useful for accurately measuring lines and angles.

Craft knife Cuts straight lines more accurately than scissors. Make sure you change the blade regularly.

Paintbrushes Save your best artist's brushes for watercolours and use cheaper brushes for varnishes, acrylic, household paints, and PVA glue.

Tweezers Use these to position small components such as jewels, sequins, and small stickers.

Iron An iron on a medium setting is used to flatten and smooth homemade paper sheets once dry.

Screen printing

Silk screens These wood or metal frames have a monofilament mesh and are used with a squeegee. A 90T mesh is standard for screen printing onto paper. The higher the number, the finer the mesh.

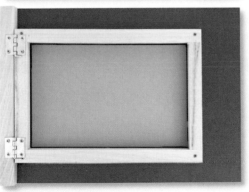

Base sheet and hinges The base sheet is attached to the screen with hinges so you can lift the screen up and down easily. The base sheet holds the card and stencil in place.

Squeegee This is used for pushing the ink through the screen onto the card. It can be made from rubber or plastic and should fit inside the frame of the silk screen. A square-edged blade is best for working on paper.

Thin acetate Use thin acetate or plastic for a durable stencil. Alternatively, you can use 70–90gsm printer paper. This will make several prints before starting to absorb the ink and becoming unuseable.

Scrubbing brush This is used for cleaning the screen once you have finished printing. Always do this as soon as you have finished printing, before the ink dries. Nylon bristles are best.

Screen printing inks There are both water- and spirit-based varieties of ink. Water-based inks are good for beginners and are easy to wash out of the screen. They come in a range of colours, which can be mixed together.

Techniques
and Projects

Papermaking TECHNIQUES

Paper has come a long way since the ancient Chinese first made paper in the second century BC. The Egyptians used papyrus, our ancestors used animal skins, but we gradually developed a process of making an even surface to write or draw on from pulped fibres. To make your own paper, use paper such as printer paper that's already been pulped once.

Making a mould and deckle

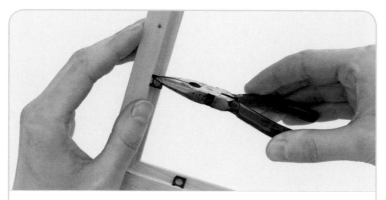

1 You will need two sturdy picture frames of roughly the same size to make a mould and deckle. If one is slightly larger, it should be the mould. Remove any hooks, clips, or wires from the frames.

2 To make the mould, stretch netting or fine mesh (plastic mosquito mesh works well) tightly across the flat side of the frame and staple all around the edge. This side is the top of the mould.

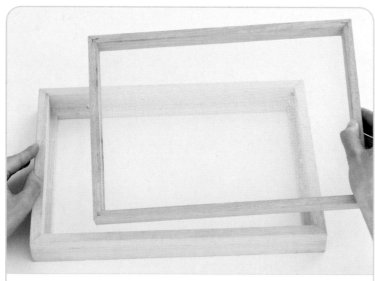

3 Hold the mould so that the netting is uppermost. Place the deckle flat side down on top of the mould. The deckle "frames" the paper pulp, forming a neat edge all round.

Selecting paper to use

Some papers work better than others for papermaking. Suitable papers include bank statements, printer paper, old letters, and other non-glossy papers without too much dark printing. Papers that aren't suitable are glossy papers, such as magazines and colour supplements, or recycled paper, such as newspapers and kitchen paper, whose fibres are too short. Try to stick to one dominant colour.

Shredding and soaking paper

Shred the paper into short 1cm (³⁄₈in) wide strips. Soak in a tub of water for at least a couple of hours – overnight is better – to allow the water to penetrate the fibres.

Building a couching mound

1 Lay some open newspapers on your work surface. Build a pile of newspapers, one folded over the next, concertina-style, about 5 to 8cm (2 to 3in) high and a little wider and longer than the mould. There should be no dip in the centre or water will pool there.

2 Drape several old towels over the mound of newspapers and roll them up around the edges. This is the "couching mound", on which you'll lay your sheets of paper to drain.

Making paper pulp

1 Half-fill a large shallow tray with cold water. Scoop some of the soaked paper into a food processor, cover with water, and blitz until it resembles a paste. Empty the paste into the tray. Repeat until the water in the tray is like a thickish soup.

Angelina fibres

2 If you're planning to add other fibres, glitter, or Angelina, stir them in now. Yarn and/or flower petals can also be added to the mix, or you can add them later if you want to control what their final position will be. Stir the mixture thoroughly.

Making paper from pulp

1 Hold the mould and deckle together, with the deckle flat side down on top. Slide them into the tray of pulp at a 45° angle. Scoop up some of the pulp. Carefully withdraw the mould and deckle, shaking gently as you do so. This will help distribute the pulp evenly, which avoids holes in the paper.

2 Let the water drain through the netting, then tilt the mould and deckle gently towards one corner to allow the excess water to run off.

3 Lift off the deckle, then carefully lay an absorbent cloth over the pulp.

4 Align the edge of the mould with the edge of the couching mound. Quickly flip the mould containing the pulp on top of the mound.

5 Run your fingers over the netting: the pulp will start to come away from the mould and stick to the cloth beneath.

6 Carefully peel away the mould. Start by lifting one corner or side: the pulp should remain on the cloth. Run your hand over any obstinate areas to help release the pulp from the net. Leave the pulp to drain.

Draining and drying the paper

1 Cover the sheet of paper with cloth and start work on the next sheet. Build up a pile of cloths and sheets, one on top of the other, on the couching mound. When the "pulp soup" gets thin, blitz some more soaked paper and add it to the pulp mix.

heavy weight

2 Once you've used up as much of the pulp as you can and before the sheets of paper get too thin, lay one final cloth and a newspaper or towel over the top of the mound. Then lay a chopping board on top, pile some weights onto it, and leave for 10 minutes to squeeze any remaining water out of the sheets.

3 Remove the weights and chopping board and carefully peel off the top cloth.

4 The sheet of paper usually adheres to the cloth beneath it. Peg it onto a line or drying rack to dry. Lift and peg each successive cloth with paper attached. Leave to dry overnight or for a few days if the weather is damp.

5 When the paper is dry, remove it from the cloth. If it doesn't come away easily, iron it with the cloth face upwards, then peel the cloth off. If the paper has curled at the edges, press it flat with a medium-hot iron.

Petal writing paper PROJECT

Make some unique and decorative paper to write a special letter to a friend or to mount a precious picture on. Handmade paper is easy to make but hard to beat when it comes to making an impression. Use paper that you would otherwise recycle and add dried petals and scraps of coloured or metallic thread to create a really special effect.

YOU WILL NEED

- paper to shred (see p.18)
- shredder
- tub
- food processor
- large shallow tray
- red or pink food colouring (optional)
- newspaper
- old towels
- mould and deckle
- dried flower petals
- short scraps of coloured thread (optional)
- absorbent cloths a little larger than the mould
- chopping board
- heavy weight
- iron

1 Shred and soak the paper. Make the pulp following **making paper pulp** on p.19. If the pulp looks greyish, stir in a little red or pink food colouring. Follow **building a couching mound** on p.19.

2 Slide the mould and deckle into the tray and scoop up some pulp. Shake to distribute the pulp evenly, then tilt the mould and deckle to allow excess water to run off.

3 Scatter dried petals around the edge of the paper so they won't obscure any writing. You may wish to scatter a little more pulp over the petals, or lay some scraps of thread over them to "fix" them to the paper.

4 Lift the deckle, then carefully place an absorbent cloth over the paper, taking care not to disturb the petals.

5 Flip the cloth and mould over onto the couching mound to drain. Run your fingers over the netting to dislodge the sheet of paper, then gently lift the mould off. Place absorbent cloth over the sheet of paper.

6 Continue making sheets until the pulp gets too thin, then drain the paper using a heavy weight on a chopping board to help squeeze out the water. Hang up to dry. When dry, iron the reverse side of the sheets, so as not to scorch or disturb the petals.

Paper marbling TECHNIQUES

Marbling is a great way to experiment with paper, colour, and pattern. Every piece of hand-marbled paper is unique, although with practice you'll be able to make similar patterns reliably. The patterns can be as simple or as complicated as you choose. Place a sheet of newspaper or a protective cloth on your work surface before you start marbling.

Preparing the size

"Size" thickens the water the paint will float on. To make it, mix wallpaper paste or marbling size with water, as directed on the packet, and pour into a large shallow tray to fill it to 2 to 3cm (approx 1in). Leave to set for about 30 minutes.

Adding the paint

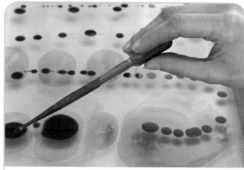

1 Load a pipette or paintbrush with acrylic or marbling paint and gently flick, drip, or trail it onto the set size. It will spread quite fast, so work quickly. If the paint sinks, thin it with a little water, shake until you reach the right consistency, and try again.

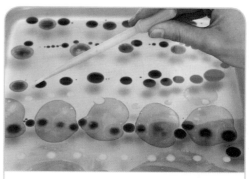

2 If you're using more than one colour, rinse the pipette or paintbrush, dry it with kitchen paper, then reload it with another colour. Flick onto the surface of the size, in between the blobs or trails of the first colour.

Creating patterns and effects

1 For a veined-marble effect, drag a cocktail stick randomly once or twice through the paint.

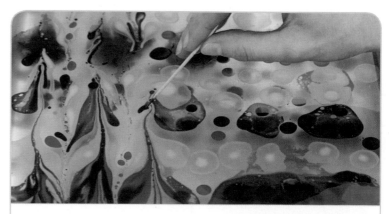

2 For a flame-like pattern, drag a cocktail stick over the surface of the paint, from one edge of the tray to the other, then move the cocktail stick towards the centre and drag it back in the opposite direction. Repeat to make more lines/rows of pattern.

3 To make more complex patterns, after Step 1, drag the cocktail stick to and fro over the surface at right angles to your first patterns to break them into smaller "flames".

4 To add a further dimension, drag a wide-tooth comb over the flames to produce a series of repeating loops. Each pattern is unique and it's great fun to experiment, but be careful not to overwork the pattern as the paints will mix together and end up looking muddy.

Marbling the paper

1 Hold the paper (120gsm is ideal) at either edge so that it dips a little in the middle. Lower it onto the paint so that the centre of the paper touches the paint first, followed by the edges. This prevents bubbles of air getting trapped underneath the paper.

2 Leave the paper for at least 10 seconds so it absorbs as much paint as possible. Then lift it out and rinse off the size under gently running cold water for a few seconds; stop if the paint starts to wash off.

3 Place the marbled paper face up on a towel to dry. Drag a sheet of kitchen paper or newspaper over the surface of the size to blot up any leftover paint, then add more paint and repeat the process to produce another sheet.

4 When the paper is dry, iron it on a medium heat to flatten it out.

Marbled book cover PROJECT

Turn an inexpensive notebook into something unique and special with a few sheets of hand-marbled paper, a little glue, and bookbinding tape. You could transform a plain hardback diary, notebook, or address book into the perfect gift.

YOU WILL NEED

- A5 hardback notebook
- 2 x A4 sheets of handmade marbled paper in matching colours (see techniques on pp.24–25)
- 1 x A4 sheet of handmade marbled paper in a contrasting colour (see techniques on pp.24–25)
- ruler
- PVA glue stick
- scissors
- craft knife
- 5cm (2in) wide bookbinding tape

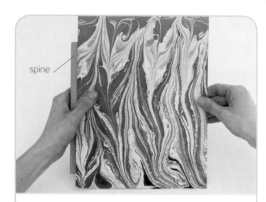

1 Slide the notebook under a sheet of marbled paper and centre the pattern on the front of the book. Leave at least 2.5cm (1in) from the edges of the sheet to the outside edges of the book.

2 Run your fingers around the outside edges and corners of the book to crease the paper. Run your thumbnail up the crease near the spine.

3 Cut the paper 2.5cm (1in) beyond the creases, and cut straight up the line made with your thumbnail. Apply PVA glue to the front cover and position the paper with the "thumbnail" crease by the spine and the other creases at the edges of the book. Press the paper to the cover and smooth it.

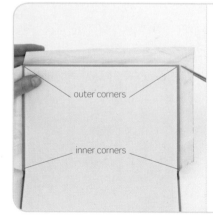

outer corners

inner corners

4 With the book open, snip the paper at an angle at the inner corners and cut away a 120° wedge at the outer corners. This ensures the paper overlaps neatly when folded to the inside.

5 Apply PVA glue around the edges of the inside cover. Fold the top and bottom edges of the marbled paper firmly onto the glue, then fold the outside edge over and smooth into position. Make sure all edges are well stuck down.

6 To neaten the inside cover, cut the contrasting sheet of marbled paper 5mm (¼in) smaller all round than the book cover. Apply PVA glue to the inside cover and stick the contrasting sheet down so that it covers the folded-over edges of the first sheet.

7 Repeat Steps 2, 3, 4, and 5, using the matching paper to make the back cover. Cut some bookbinding tape 2cm (¾in) longer than the spine. Lay it flat on your work surface, sticky-side up, centre the spine, then press the spine on the tape. Turn the book to one side and smooth the tape around the corner onto the flat surface; it should overlap onto the marbled paper. Repeat for the other side. Crease the tape either side of the spine.

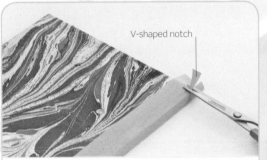

V-shaped notch

8 Cut V-shaped notches in the tape at the top and bottom of the spine indents and fold it over the front and back cover. You may be able to fold the tape in at the spine in the same way; if there isn't space, trim the tape and fold it over on itself to avoid a raw edge.

9 To make the corners, cut four 5cm (2in) lengths of bookbinding tape. Place one sticky-side up on the work surface. With the book open, position one corner diagonally over the tape so that a triangle of tape shows on either side, with a sliver of about 1mm (¹⁄₁₆in) still visible at the tip to allow for the thickness of the cover. Press the cover onto the tape, then fold the triangles to the inside cover. They should just about meet in the middle. Repeat for all corners.

Papier-mâché TECHNIQUES

The term papier-mâché is French for "chewed paper", and describes a variety of techniques where paper is saturated with paste and moulded into a shape which, when dry, forms a hard, durable shell. It is remarkable what a magical transformation can be achieved with old newspapers and paste, which makes papier-mâché a great recycling craft, ideal for creating decorative objects for the home such as vases, bowls, boxes, pencil pots, plaques, and trays.

Making a base

1 Select suitable plastic or cardboard containers that can be joined together to create interesting, one-off shapes.

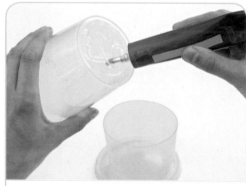

2 Use an all-purpose glue to join the components together.

3 Use plastic bags, rolled into sausages or crumpled up, to pad out the basic form. Stick these in place with sticky tape.

Preparing the papier-mâché

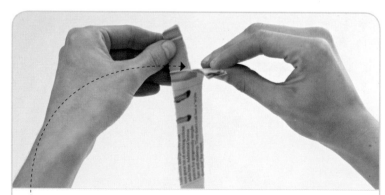

1 The paper should be absorbent: use old newspapers or pages torn from telephone directories. Tear the paper into manageable strips – don't cut it; the torn edges, when overlapped, will form a smooth surface without too many ridges.

2 Mix wallpaper paste in a bowl, following the instructions on the packet. Most pastes contain fungicides, so if you have sensitive skin, you may wish to wear rubber gloves. Protect your work surface with newspaper or plastic sheeting.

Building layers

1 It's important to ensure that each paper strip is saturated with wallpaper paste. Dip it into the paste and use your fingers to remove surplus paste.

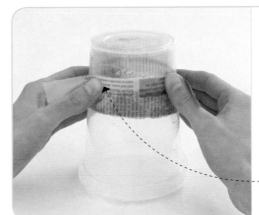

2 Apply the paper strip to the object and smooth it out with your fingertips, expelling air bubbles. Make sure you cover not only the surfaces but also all the edges and joins.

3 Build up lots of layers – at least eight or nine – to ensure a successful result.

tissue paper

4 Newsprint creates a neutral grey surface but if you wish to cover this up, apply a few layers of tissue paper; this will help to disguise the print and also creates a smoother surface.

Decorating the object

1 Allow the papier-mâché to dry completely before decorating. If there are any ridges or bumps, lightly sand the surface using fine sandpaper.

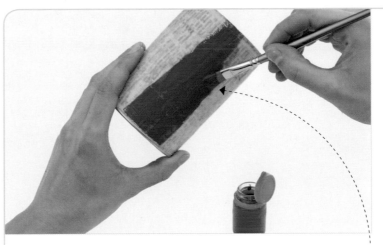

2 If you wish to decorate the surface of the papier-mâché object, you can paint it with water-based paints such as poster paints, watercolours, gouache, acrylics, or even household emulsion. Apply an (optional) undercoat of white paint if you want to use very light colours.

3 Once you have decorated the item, finish by sealing it with several coats of water-based varnish.

Papier-mâché bowl PROJECT

This decorative bowl is made from a disposable plastic receptacle – the kind sold in supermarkets containing salads – and the cardboard plinth from the centre of a ball of knitting yarn, plus a couple of plastic bags to pad out the rim. You can create a stylish bowl from these humble components, and decorate the surface using coloured tissue paper and a smattering of metal leaf.

YOU WILL NEED

- plastic bowl
- cardboard cylinder
- all-purpose glue
- 1–2 plastic bags
- sticky tape
- card
- scissors
- wallpaper paste
- newspaper, torn into strips
- PVA glue
- medium and large soft paintbrushes
- coloured tissue papers
- metal leaf size
- metal leaf
- water-based varnish

1 Glue the cardboard cylinder to the base of the bowl. Roll up one or two plastic bags and tape them under the rim of the bowl. Cut a circle of card to fit the base of the cylinder and glue or tape it in place.

2 Mix up wallpaper paste. Dip strips of newspaper in the paste, squeeze off excess paste with your fingers, and apply the saturated strips to the inside and outside of the bowl and all over the plinth, smoothing out each strip as you go.

3 Continue in this way until the whole piece is covered, then repeat until you have built up at least eight or nine layers. Leave to dry completely (this can take several days or even weeks, depending on temperature and humidity).

4 Once dry, brush the surface of the entire piece with PVA diluted with water to the consistency of single cream, then apply pieces of coloured tissue paper, brushing each one with diluted PVA. Apply two or three layers of tissue, then leave to dry.

5 Cut out circles from tissue paper in a contrasting colour, and glue these in place, using more of the diluted PVA. Leave to dry for several hours or overnight.

6 Once the tissue layers are dry, paint the rim with metal leaf size. Leave for 10 minutes, then apply metal leaf over the size, rubbing down gently with clean fingers. Use a large, soft brush to brush away any excess. Protect with two or three coats of varnish.

Piñata party PROJECT

Piñatas are a fun addition to birthday parties and festivals. Stuffed with sweets and toys, the piñata is hung from a tree and children take turns to hit it with a stick until the sweets and toys are released. Traditionally made of papier mâché in shapes from donkeys to footballs and even dinosaurs, our owl piñata is quick and easy to make from a balloon and coloured tissue paper.

YOU WILL NEED

- balloon
- PVA glue
- newspaper, cut into strips
- coloured tissue paper and card
- scissors
- pencil
- string
- sweets and toys

1 Fully inflate a large balloon – this will form the base of your piñata. Tie a knot to secure. Glue 3cm (1¼in)-wide strips of newspaper all over the balloon, leaving an uncovered area around the knot.

2 Leave the papier-mâché to dry, then repeat the process by sticking on two more layers. Pop the balloon with a pin and trim away the knot with scissors so you are left with a shell.

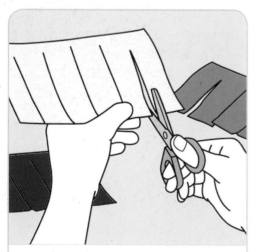

3 Cut the tissue paper into strips and make slits along the edge to form fringing. Glue the layers of paper to the papier-mâché shell, starting from the bottom, where the balloon's knot used to be.

4 Cut out two eyes using yellow and black card, a yellow beak, two pink feet, and two elliptical wings. Glue the pieces of card to the shell and use more tissue paper to decorate the rest of the owl.

5 Make two small holes in the top of the piñata with a pencil lead. Thread a long piece of string through a large-eyed needle and push it through one hole and out through the other. Tie in a knot to form a loop.

6 Fill the owl with sweets and small plastic toys through the gap in the base of the shell. Cut a piece of card big enough to cover the hole. Use tape to keep it in place and then hang up your owl.

Scrapbooking TECHNIQUES

For decades, even centuries, people have enjoyed preserving paper scraps, tickets, greetings cards, postcards, and other memorabilia in albums. The new generation of scrapbooks are, essentially, highly decorated personalized photograph albums. The vast array of scrapbooking materials for sale in most craft shops and online is an indication that the craft is enjoying a huge revival. Here are some tips on how to make a basic scrapbook page to which you can add your own personal touches.

Choosing materials

1 A photograph or other image forms the focal point of an album page. Use a colour or theme from the photograph when selecting papers to form the background of the page. Materials with a high acid content will deteriorate over time, so make sure you use acid-free papers and card, as well as a suitable acid-free adhesive.

2 If you can't find paper of a suitable colour, make your own. Use water-based paints – watercolours, gouache, or acrylics – to paint a wash on white acid-free paper.

Cropping images

1 Photographs are the focal points and need to be shown to their best advantage. Use two L-shaped pieces of card to help decide how to crop pictures to eliminate distracting clutter.

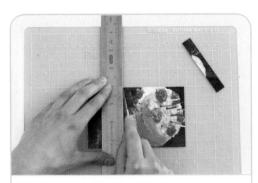

2 Once you have decided on the format for your photograph, use a steel ruler and a craft knife to trim off unwanted areas. Protect your work surface by using a cutting mat.

3 Enhance pictures by sticking them onto pieces of card that are bigger than the image, forming a border all round. Experiment with edging tools to create decorative borders.

Making a border

1 Look out for decorative papers with printed borders that can be cut out for special pictures. As when selecting a background, choose harmonious colours.

2 Use small sharp scissors to cut out intricate shapes. Once you have cut out your border pieces, place them on the photograph to see if adjustments are needed.

3 Use a suitable acid-free adhesive to stick your photograph onto the background, then stick the border in place, trimming off any excess paper where pieces overlap.

Making embellishments

decorative punch

Craft supply shops are well stocked with ready-made embellishments but you can make your own, cutting out paper shapes freehand with scissors or using a decorative punch. This is a great way to utilize paper scraps left over from other projects.

Applying brads and eyelets

Punch a hole through all layers of paper where you wish to apply a brad or eyelet. Brads can be added by hand – just insert into the hole and spread out the metal prongs on the reverse. To add an eyelet, use a special setting tool and a hammer.

Making a hinge

A strip of paper with one end glued to the background makes a good hinge. You could fold the paper to create a concertina, which is useful for a series of pictures or a long caption that wouldn't otherwise fit across the width of the page.

Hidden journalling

"Journalling" refers to words, usually in the form of captions, stories, or poems. If these are personal or too long to fit on the page, write or print them on a separate piece of paper and fold it, then place it in an envelope glued to the background. This is a useful device for any items that you wouldn't wish to glue directly to the page.

Scrapbook page PROJECT

Old family photographs are the starting point for this scrapbooking project, which uses printed papers and a range of simple but effective techniques to create a nostalgic atmosphere that will stand the test of time. Use these step-by-step instructions only as a rough guide, adding your own creative touches to make your scrapbook really personal.

YOU WILL NEED

- ring binder scrapbook with plain pages
- old family photographs or postcards
- plain and printed papers
- metal ruler
- craft knife
- cutting mat
- glue stick
- self-adhesive paper lace
- photo corners (optional)
- dimensional decorative stickers
- ribbon
- small envelope
- rubber stamp and ink pad

1 Gather all your materials together before you begin. Once you have selected the photographs you wish to use, choose papers and other materials such as stickers, ribbons, labels, and rubber stamps that suit the theme and colour scheme.

2 Cut printed papers to fit the dimensions of the page and stick these in place. For best effect, also arrange some slightly smaller contrasting papers on top to make a multi-dimensional backdrop. Glue in place.

3 To make a frame, cut self-adhesive paper lace longer than the frame you wish to create. Peel off the backing and stick in place, with the ends overlapping at corners. Make diagonal cuts across the corners, then peel away the excess to form a neat mitre.

4 Once the frames are in place, stick down the photographs. If they are originals, you may wish to use photo corners to avoid damaging the paper; or make photocopies and stick these down. Add a sticker to each corner of the frame.

5 Add more stickers and tie a handmade label to the top of the ring binder with ribbon. Apply glue to the front of an envelope and stick it onto the page, then slip in a sheet of paper with your "secret journalling" (see p.35). A rubber-stamped heart on the flap adds a final flourish.

Lino printing TECHNIQUES

Lino printing can produce a similar effect to a traditional woodcut but lino is easier to carve than wood. The parts you cut away remain the colour of the surface you are printing on and uncut areas create the printing surface. Remember when you transfer your design to the lino that it will be reversed once it is printed. Cut away enough lino to create clear areas of print surface: lines that are too thin will become clogged with ink and may not print clearly.

Transferring your design

1 A simple design can be drawn straight onto the surface of the lino using a soft pencil. Make sure that the lino is clean and free from grease and dust. Alternatively, you may prefer to draw your design on paper first; this is useful if tracing a design from a printed source. Choose a thin, smooth paper such as tracing paper or layout paper.

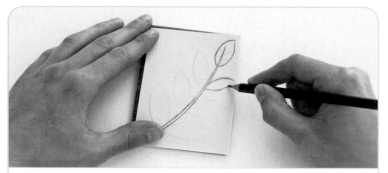

2 Place a piece of carbon paper face down on the lino and place your drawing face down on top of the carbon. You should be able to see the lines of your drawing. Trace over these lines using a hard pencil to transfer the drawing onto the surface of the lino.

Cutting lino

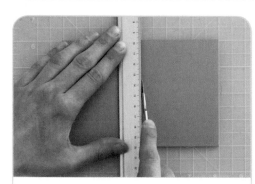

1 Lino can be bought ready-cut, but if you want a particular size, place the lino on a cutting mat and use a metal ruler and craft knife to make several shallow cuts into the lino until you have cut right through it.

2 The lino has a hessian backing. If you fold the cut lino, you can cut through the hessian. You can use a craft knife for this step or you may prefer to use scissors.

3 When it comes to cutting the design, use a narrow V-shaped gouge for thin lines. Be sure to cut these lines deeply enough, so that they do not become clogged with ink when you come to print your design.

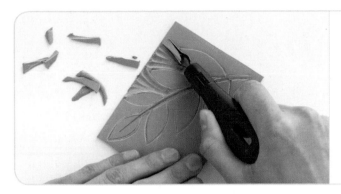

4 A U-shaped gouge is perfect for clearing large areas. Once you have finished cutting the design, brush away all the scraps of lino and make sure the printing surface is clean and dust-free.

SAFETY FIRST

It is advisable to work on a non-slip surface when cutting lino. Always cut away from you and don't put your hand in the path of lino cutters, knives, or other sharp tools.

Printing

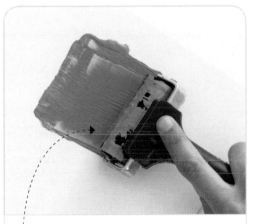

1 Roll out lino printing inks on a wipe-clean surface, such as a sheet of glass or a ceramic tile. Water-based inks are the best choice for most purposes and colours can be mixed to create the desired shade.

2 Once the roller is covered with an even layer of ink, roll it across the surface of the lino cut until it is evenly coated.

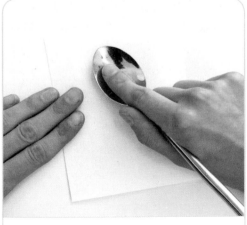

3 Place the paper on top of the inked lino and rub gently with the curved bowl of a spoon, or similar object, to press the ink onto the paper.

4 Carefully peel away the paper from the lino to reveal the print. This is the time to assess your print and decide whether or not you wish to cut away more of the lino.

Adding another colour

1 Once you have made the desired number of prints in your first colour, you can add a second colour. Wipe the ink from the surface and cut away more of the design.

2 Mix a second colour, darker than the first, then roll the inky roller over the lino.

3 Press the printed paper onto the lino, making sure the design lines up. Peel away the paper to reveal the two-colour print.

Paper decorations TECHNIQUES

For parties and festivals the world over, people love to use decorations to create an atmosphere of celebration – and paper and card are the ideal choice. It's amazing how you can transform your home with tissue paper, string, scraps of card, and some deft snips of your scissors. Use the techniques on this page, along with your own imagination and creativity, to make stunning decorations, whatever the occasion.

Concertina folding

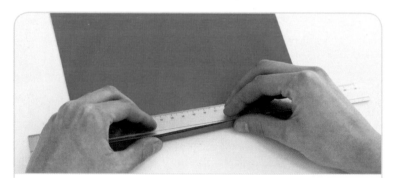

1 This basic paper-folding method is useful for all kinds of projects, such as the tissue paper pompoms on pp.44–45. Position a ruler across a sheet of paper to determine the width of the fold, then fold the paper against the edge of the ruler. Run over the fold with a blunt object to make sure it is really crisp.

2 Flip the paper over and repeat the folding process. Continue until the whole sheet has been folded into a concertina. You can create a number of decorative effects by tying a length of ribbon around the folded paper, then fanning out the folds above and below.

Making paper bunting

1 Bunting is a great way to use paper scraps left over from other projects – you can even use pages cut from magazines and brochures. Fold over one edge of the paper then cut out triangle shapes on a cutting mat, using a metal ruler and craft knife.

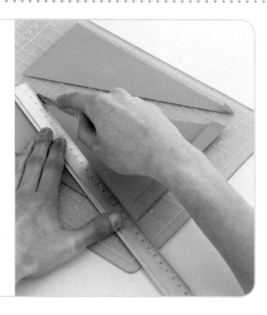

double-sided tape

2 Open out the fold and lay a strip of double-sided sticky tape across it. Lay a length of string or cord just below the tape, then peel off the tape backing, and fold the paper over, pressing to stick down the flap.

Making cardboard cutouts

1 Even the most humble, everyday materials can be transformed into decorations. Draw shapes on cardboard and cut them out with a craft knife.

2 Punch a hole in each cardboard cutout. Thread a length of string or cord through the hole and tie in a knot, ready for hanging up.

3 Use dimensional paints and gems to decorate each cutout.

Making temporary decorations

1 Make a template of a simple shape – such as a flower – then draw around the template on the paper backing of decorative self-adhesive paper or foil, then cut out the shape.

2 Peel off the paper backing and stick the shapes onto mirrors, vases, windowpanes, and other objects, as temporary decorations that can be peeled off.

Making paper "straw"

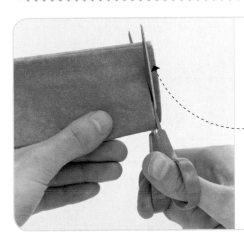

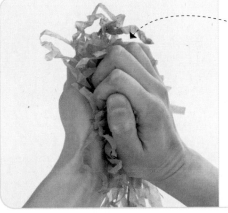

1 Fold a sheet of tissue paper several times, until it is a manageable size but not too thick, then cut across it into very thin strips.

2 Fluff out the strips, pick them up, and gently crumple them in your hands, then tease them out again. Use the resulting "straw" to line gift boxes (see pp.82–83) or as a nest for small gifts, baubles, or other decorations.

Tissue paper pompoms PROJECT

Tissue paper seems so fragile but it is more robust than it appears and is the ideal choice for bold decorations for parties and festivals. These paper balls – reminiscent of giant dandelion seed heads – can be suspended from the ceiling or from tree branches on invisible threads, or used as a table centrepiece. They will withstand a gentle breeze indoors or outdoors, though not strong winds or rain. Choose colours to match your theme.

YOU WILL NEED

- sheets of coloured tissue paper, 76 x 50cm (30 x 20in)
- scissors or craft knife
- ruler
- spoon, or similar smooth object
- 50cm (20in) lengths of florists' wire
- invisible thread

1 To make a small pompom, fold a sheet of tissue paper in half, in half again, and in half once more. You will have eight layers. Cut along the folds using scissors or a craft knife to make eight sheets measuring 25 x 19cm (10 x 7½in). Place the sheets in a neat stack.

2 Starting at one short end, make concertina folds at intervals of about 1.2cm (½in). Crease each fold as you make it by running the bowl of a spoon or the handle of your scissors along its length.

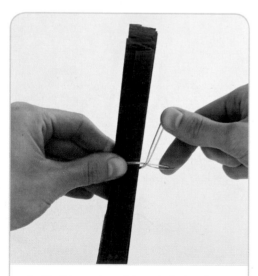

3 Bind the centre of the strip by bending a length of wire in half and twisting it firmly around the paper. Form a loop with the wire and tuck in the ends so they don't protrude.

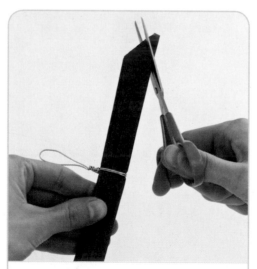

4 Cut the ends of the strip in a pointed or curved shape, depending on the effect you wish to create.

5 Use your fingertips to tease out the folds of tissue, one at a time, working towards the centre, to form a ball shape. Tie a length of invisible thread to the wire loop, for hanging.

6 To make a larger version, use eight whole sheets of tissue paper, placed on top of each other in a neat stack. Follow the instructions for the smaller version but make the folds slightly wider – about 2.5cm (1in).

Folded napkins PROJECT

Paper folding is an age-old craft that used here transforms two-dimensional plain paper napkins into stunning table decoration to impress any guest. Added embellishments also create a touch of fun. To achieve best results, crease the folds accurately and firmly with your fingers, or use a bone folder if you have one, as wonky creases may make the napkins fall over.

YOU WILL NEED

- different coloured layered paper napkins (each folded project will need two napkins)
- bone folder (optional)
- charms and accents, such as round, heart-shaped, and star-shaped sequins, flat-backed gems, small ribbon bows
- PVA or glue stick (if your embellishments are not self-adhesive)

1 Open out two different coloured paper napkins and place one on top of the other, lining up the edges. Fold them in half twice.

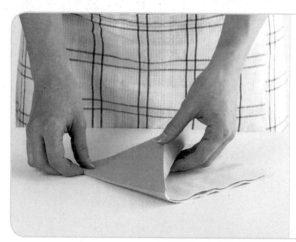

2 Carefully pick up the top loose corner of the first napkin and fold it underneath to make a pocket. Press the fold firmly to create a defined crease.

3 Repeat this process by folding the other layers. Leave a 1cm (½in) strip of paper between each fold to create a striped effect.

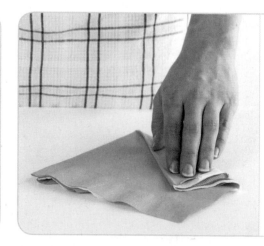

4 Turn the napkins over and fold the two side corners into the centre to create a cone shape. Firmly crease the folds to ensure that the folded napkin does not unfold.

5 Decorate each folded napkin by sticking on individual gems, glitters, ribbon bows and sparkles. Self-adhesive embellishments are cleaner to use but gluing them on works just as well. Open the pocket to place your cutlery inside. Fold additional designs, following **concertina folding** on p.42.

Drink mixers PROJECT

Brighten a party cocktail with fancy drink mixers. These jolly embellishments are made by layering card and paper, and then decorating them with sequins and beads that will catch the light as the mixers move. Once you have created the projects shown here, try making different shapes, such as animals, plants, or fruit shapes.

YOU WILL NEED

- scissors
- papers, fabric, and poster board in different colours
- glue stick or double-sided sticky tape
- selection of straws
- sequins and gems

1 To create the star mixer, cut out two plain blue star shapes and stick them back to back to the top of a straw using the glue stick. Leave the glue to dry before adding the decoration. You may wish to place the star under a weight or inside a book to obtain a firm bond.

2 Cut three smaller star shapes out of different patterned craft paper or fabric – they need to get progressively smaller. Stick them on top of the base star to create a layered effect. Add star sequins to the smallest star to finish.

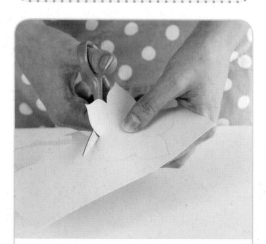

3 For the flower mixer, cut a flower shape out of poster board or craft paper. Alternatively, use a shaped punch, or cut around a template. Cut out a smaller flower to stick on top.

4 Cut another two smaller flowers and add a heart or similar shaped gem in the centre. Add silver and green sequins around the central motif and leave to dry. Glue the flower to the top of the straw.

5 For the butterfly mixer, cut out two butterfly shapes and bend the wings inwards. Glue them on top of the straw, back to back, and with their antennae aligning.

6 Cut out a selection of large and small flowers and dots, and glue them to the wings of the butterfly. Cut out six body shapes, getting progressively smaller, and glue these to either side of the butterfly's body. Decorate the edges of the wings with sparkly gems or tiny dots of glitter.

Paper hearts PROJECT

It's worth collecting all sorts of attractive or colourful papers to make child-friendly tree decorations at Christmas. Look out for wallpaper samples, pages from magazines, and old oddments of wrapping paper. Refer to **making cardboard cutouts** on p.43 when cutting out the card. Use a sharp knife and a self-healing cutting mat.

YOU WILL NEED

- pen or pencil
- paper in festive colours
- white card
- glue stick
- scissors or craft knife
- cutting mat
- length of string
- 1 decorative bead or button

1 Draw a heart, star, or alternative outline shape of your choice on a piece of decorative paper. Using a craft knife, cut out a piece of card roughly the same size as the piece of paper.

2 Glue the piece of recycled card onto the back of the paper and leave to one side for a while for the glue to dry completely.

3 Cut out the paper shape neatly using a sharp pair of scissors. Trim the shape if necessary so that no pen or pencil marks are showing.

4 Thread both ends of the string through a bead or button to create a loop. Glue the string loop to the back of the card and allow to dry.

Butterfly kite PROJECT

An ideal project to make with a child during the school summer holidays, or as a gift to celebrate a birthday or festival, this kite is made from tissue paper. Do not fly it in strong winds or the paper may tear. Alternatively, it makes a great decoration when hung on a child's bedroom wall.

YOU WILL NEED

- split canes or basketweaving reed, soaked overnight to make them flexible
- all-purpose glue
- tissue paper
- cotton thread
- kite string

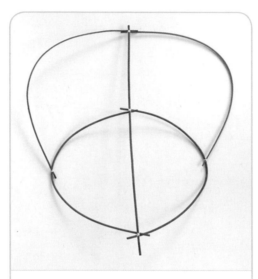

1 Wrap thread around two canes 5cm (2in) from the ends. Bend one towards the middle and secure in place with thread. Attach a cane to the other side and two more to the top.

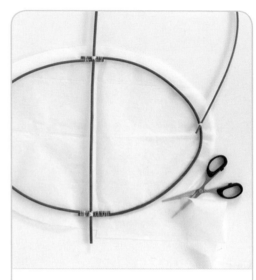

2 Put glue onto the bottom half of your frame and lay it on tissue paper, glue side down. Once dry, cut around the frame leaving a 5cm (2in) border.

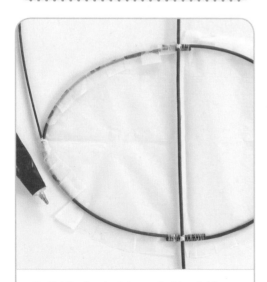

3 Cut the border into small strips, fold over and glue in place. Repeat this process for the top half. Where the two pieces meet, trim the paper and glue to the cane.

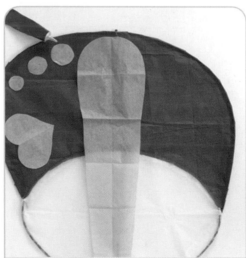

4 Cut out a strip of tissue paper for the butterfly's body and glue in place. Add other shapes to decorate the wings. Add two eyes.

5 Cut and fold five strips of tissue paper and staple together. Glue to the bottom of the kite. Cut two lengths of kite string 5cm (2in) longer than your kite.

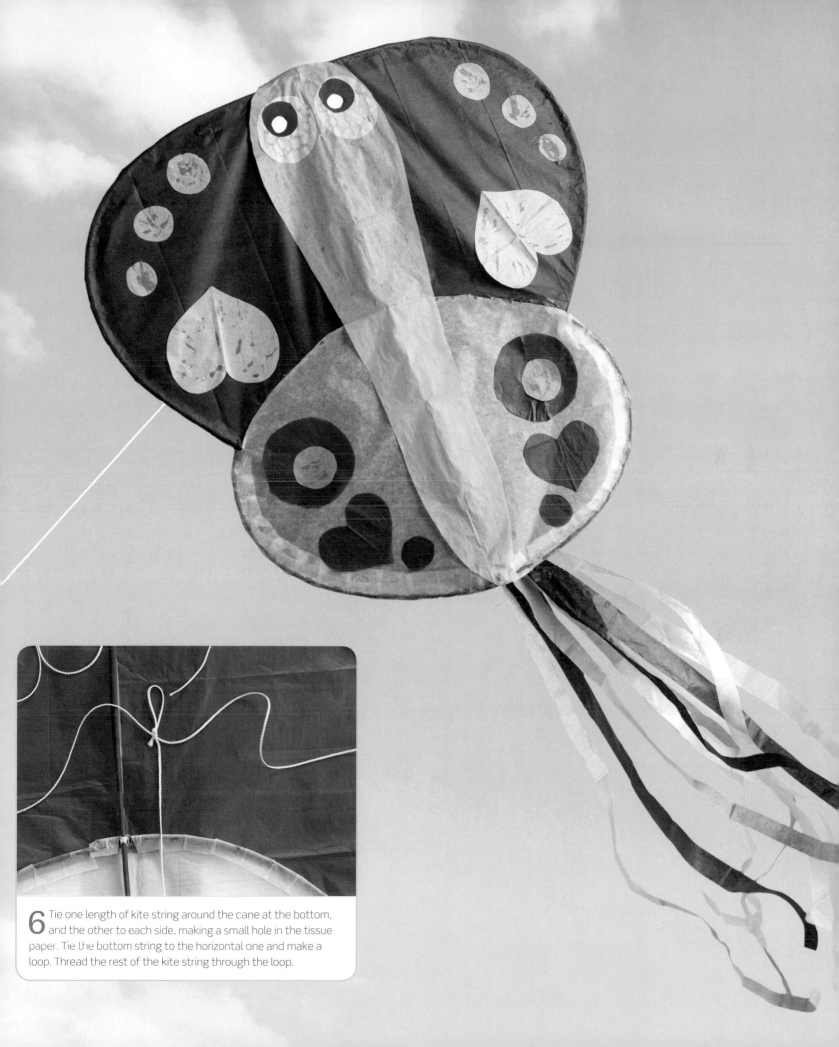

6 Tie one length of kite string around the cane at the bottom, and the other to each side, making a small hole in the tissue paper. Tie the bottom string to the horizontal one and make a loop. Thread the rest of the kite string through the loop.

Origami animals PROJECT

Origami is the traditional Japanese art of folding paper to create intricate sculptures. Make a selection of animals, shown below, simply by folding the paper as shown – no cutting or glueing is required! Practise makes perfect, so treat your first few attempts as trial creatures before successfully mastering a fox and a pig. You can then use your origami as ornaments or dinner party settings.

YOU WILL NEED

- origami paper square
- paper folder (optional)
- sticker eyes

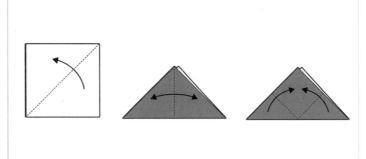

1 To make the fox, fold your paper in half diagonally to form a triangle. Fold the paper in half diagonally again to make a smaller triangle. Now fold the bottom two corners inwards to meet the centre line.

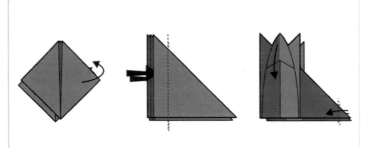

2 Fold your diamond shaped paper in half to create a triangle. Rotate the paper. Open the left edge to form ears. Fold down the central layer to form the head. Fold the corner of the triangle to form a tail. Add sticker eyes.

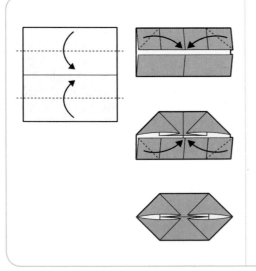

1 To make the pig, fold your paper in half, then fold the top and bottom edges in to meet at the central crease. Fold the front left and right corners, and invert. Repeat for the back. Turn over your paper so that the folds are facing away from you ready for the next step.

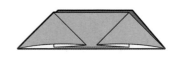

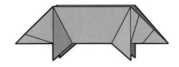

2 Fold the paper shape in half along its length. Fold the triangle flaps outwards and repeat for all four flaps – these will form the legs. Invert each end, using the solid lines as guides to form the snout and tail.

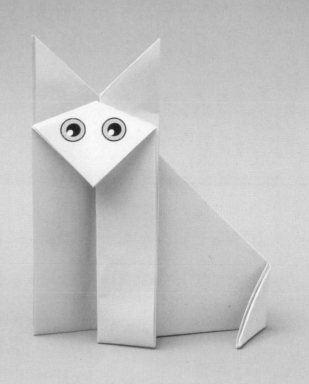

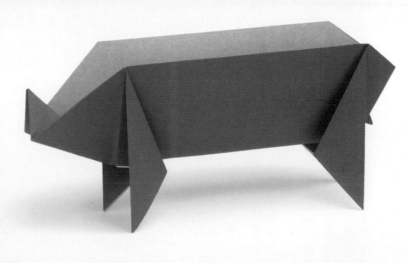

Découpage TECHNIQUES

Découpage is the craft of decorating an object with paper cutouts glued in place. If you take the time to apply many coats of varnish over the paper cutouts, they will appear to sink into the surface and will look as though they are part of the object and not merely stuck on. Choose from the wide range of printed papers available: gift wrap, magazine pages, catalogues, and brochures – and even papers with repeat motifs printed specifically for découpage.

Choosing your materials

Look for papers that have printed motifs that are separate and do not overlap with other parts of the design. This will provide you with individual elements to cut out. Make sure you have enough of your chosen motifs: buy two or more sheets of paper, if necessary.

Cutting out the motifs

1 Rough-cut the paper: this means cutting out each motif roughly, leaving a border of paper all round.

2 Using small scissors with pointed blades to ensure accuracy, cut out each motif very carefully. For best results, keep the scissors quite static and move the paper, rather than the other way round.

3 Make sure you cut away any areas of background within the motif. This is particularly important if, say, the background is white and the object you are sticking the motif onto is coloured.

Arranging and glueing the cutouts

1 Try out your design before sticking anything down. Move the cutouts around until you are happy with the arrangement.

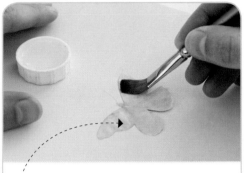

2 Brush découpage medium or PVA glue diluted with water to the consistency of thin cream onto the back of each cutout. Make sure each piece is thoroughly covered and there are no dry areas.

3 Place the glued cutouts in place and smooth out the paper, expelling any air bubbles. Use the same brush you used to apply the medium to the back of the cutouts.

Varnishing the piece

When the cutout is stuck down, leave it to dry, then apply a coat of clear varnish. You can choose a matt or gloss varnish, depending on the effect you want to achieve. Apply several coats of varnish, allowing each one to dry before applying the next.

Adding embellishments

1 To highlight small areas of the design, stick on flat-backed gems, which will add texture and sparkle.

2 Glitter also adds a touch of sparkle to a finished design. Simply apply dabs of glue using a cocktail stick to the areas you wish to highlight.

glitter

3 Then sprinkle on glitter, tip off any excess, and leave to dry thoroughly.

Keepsake box PROJECT

You can use découpage to decorate a number of different objects. A plain cardboard box is an ideal candidate for this technique. Choose one that is sturdy and well-proportioned, and look for printed papers with attractive flower heads and leaves – such as these pansies – to combine into an elegant floral arrangement to decorate the lid and sides of the box.

YOU WILL NEED

- printed papers
- small scissors with pointed blades
- cardboard box with lid
- soft paintbrush
- découpage medium or PVA glue diluted with water to the consistency of thin cream
- water-based gloss varnish

1 Cut out motifs roughly from printed paper then, using small scissors, cut out each one neatly, including areas between the leaves, stems, and petals.

2 Arrange the cutouts on the box until you are satisfied with the design. Take time to assess whether you have enough cutouts or whether you need to make more.

back of cutout

3 Using a soft paintbrush, apply découpage medium or diluted PVA glue all over the back of the cutout that will form the basis of your arrangement.

4 Place the pasted cutout in position on the box lid and smooth out, using the brush still loaded with medium. Repeat to complete the arrangement with the remaining cutouts.

5 Apply cutouts to the sides of the box in a similar way, avoiding the upper part which will be covered by the sides of the lid.

6 To protect the paper cutouts and to create an attractive finish, brush the box with several coats of varnish – ideally about six or more coats – leaving each coat to dry thoroughly before applying the next.

Paper punching TECHNIQUES

Punching is a decorative technique that is used to add patterns to paper and thin card. Not all papers punch successfully: mulberry papers, tissue paper, and some natural fibre papers are too soft. Punches won't punch through paper or card that is too thick either, so try out your punch on sample papers first to ensure a good result.

Making a template for a conical lampshade

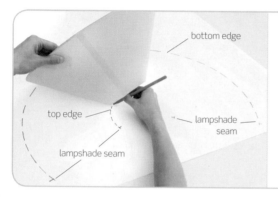

1 Place the lampshade on a large piece of paper with the seam aligned near the long edge of the paper. Mark the position of the seam, then roll the lampshade, marking the trajectory of the bottom edge with a pencil, until you get to the seam again. Mark the position of the seam at the other end. Roll the shade again as before, this time marking the top edge and seam.

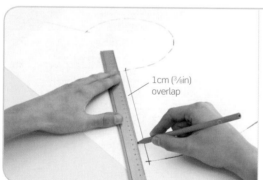

2 Draw a smooth curve along the top and bottom trajectory lines. Join the seam marks with a ruler, adding a 1cm (³⁄₈in) overlap at one end. Cut along the lines.

3 Check the size and shape of the sleeve by placing it over the lampshade. Make any necessary adjustments, then use as a template to cut the coloured paper sleeve.

Punching

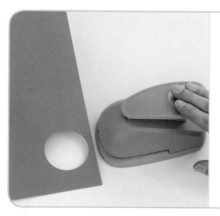

1 Most punches have a slot for the paper and a lever to punch the shape. Standard punches punch close to the edge of the paper; long-arm punches punch further in from the edge. Working on a flat surface, slot the paper into the punch, and press the lever firmly.

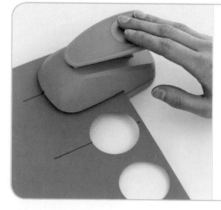

2 To space punched shapes accurately, use the side of the punch as a guide (align the edge of the punch with the edge of the previous shape, for example) or mark with a pencil before starting. You may need to mark the punch too to position it accurately.

3 To punch a shape out of patterned paper or to position text in the centre of a shape, turn the punch upside down. Slot the paper into the punch so that you can see the pattern positioned correctly, then press the lever.

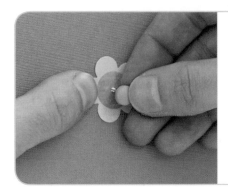

4 Punching creates an aperture as well as a cut-out shape. Use the shape as an embellishment: stick it onto a background, or punch a small hole through the shape and the background, and insert a brad or eyelet to secure.

Using an "anywhere" punch

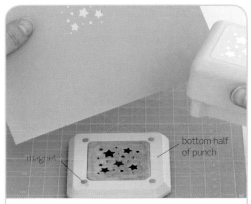

bottom half of punch

magnet

1 Larger "anywhere" punches use magnets to align the top and bottom halves of the punch on the paper. Place the bottom half on a cutting mat, then place the paper on top. Lower the top half until the magnets attract and the punch is positioned exactly.

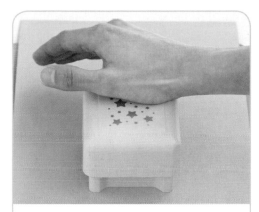

2 Press the top half of the punch with the heel of your hand, or preferably with both hands. If the punch is not lined up correctly it won't punch. Lift off the top half of the punch to see the punched shape.

3 "Anywhere" punches can punch at any angle: either rotate the base of the punch to the required position or turn the paper. When punching shapes close together, make sure you don't punch into a previous shape.

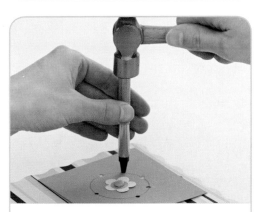

4 To punch a hole anywhere on a surface, use a hammer punch and mat. The tips are interchangeable for different sizes of holes. Use a special punching mat as this type of punch will damage a regular cutting mat.

5 Spring-loaded eyelet punches can punch holes anywhere. Position the punch on the paper with a punching mat underneath, pull up to tension the spring, and release. The spring creates a hammer action that punches a hole in the paper.

Looking after your punches

Punches need some maintenance. If the punch sticks, punch through several layers of wax paper to lubricate it. If the punch is blunt, punch repeatedly through several layers of aluminium foil to sharpen it.

Punched lampshade PROJECT

A plain white lampshade can be transformed by covering it with a coloured paper sleeve. Add interest by punching holes in the paper so that the colour of the lampshade shows through. Here, a pretty star punch was used to create a night sky effect on fabulous lavender blue paper, but there are lots of different punch designs that could be used on other colours of paper.

YOU WILL NEED

- plain lampshade
- white paper for the template
- pencil
- ruler
- lavender blue paper
- scissors
- 4cm (1½in) starry night "anywhere" punch, see p.61
- eraser
- double-sided sticky tape

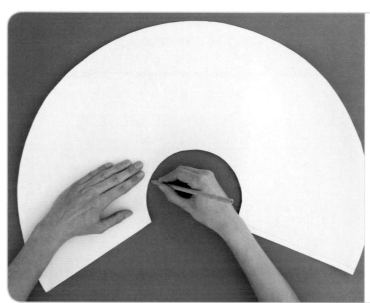

1 Follow **making a template for a conical lampshade** on p.60. Use the resulting template on the right side of the lavender blue paper to make the lampshade sleeve. Mark the 1cm (³⁄₈in) overlap at one end on the coloured paper then cut out.

2 Following **using an "anywhere" punch** on p.61, punch around the entire bottom edge of the sleeve, marking each start point 4cm (1½in) – or the size of your punch – from the last with a light pencil mark.

one-third mark

3 Fold the white template into thirds and use it to pencil mark the right side of the coloured sleeve into thirds. Cut a number of 4cm (1½in) squares and arrange them in a regular and/or random pattern on the first third of the sleeve. Draw light pencil lines around each square.

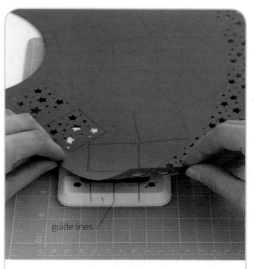

guide lines

4 Line the punch up with one of the marked squares. You can mark the edges of the punch for accurate positioning. Hold the paper while you align the punch with the horizontal and vertical lines of the marked square. Punch the shape. Repeat to punch each square.

5 Work around the sleeve, marking more squares on each third of the sleeve. Once all the squares have been punched, rub out the pencil lines. Using double-sided sticky tape, stick the overlap under the edge of the seam. Place the sleeve over the lampshade.

seam

Glowing angels PROJECT

Paper lanterns are great for decorating a garden or just lighting up a path or driveway when hosting a celebration, or holiday party. Paper-cut angels make these lanterns even more special as the outlines glow in the dark while the candles shine through the punched holes. Never leave a candle unattended indoors.

YOU WILL NEED

- white or plain coloured paper
- glass or see-through tealight holder
- pencil
- ruler
- scissors
- hole punch
- sticky tape
- tealights or small candles

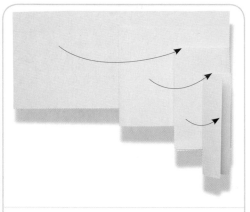

1 Wrap the paper around a tealight holder. Cut it to size so it fits around the holder with a small overlap while the top reaches just above the rim of the holder. Fold the paper as indicated by the arrows.

2 Draw a design on the folded paper and cut it out. You may need to practice drawing the outlines on a spare piece of paper in order that the cut-out shape transforms into the outline you intend. We've used angels but this method works for all sorts of images.

3 Open out the folded paper to reveal a row of angels with their wings outstretched. Use a single hole punch to carefully add circular "dots" along the edges of each angel's wings.

4 Fold the paper into a cylinder shape and tape the ends together. Slip the decoration over the tealight holder – it should fit snugly around the glass. Place a tealight inside the holder.

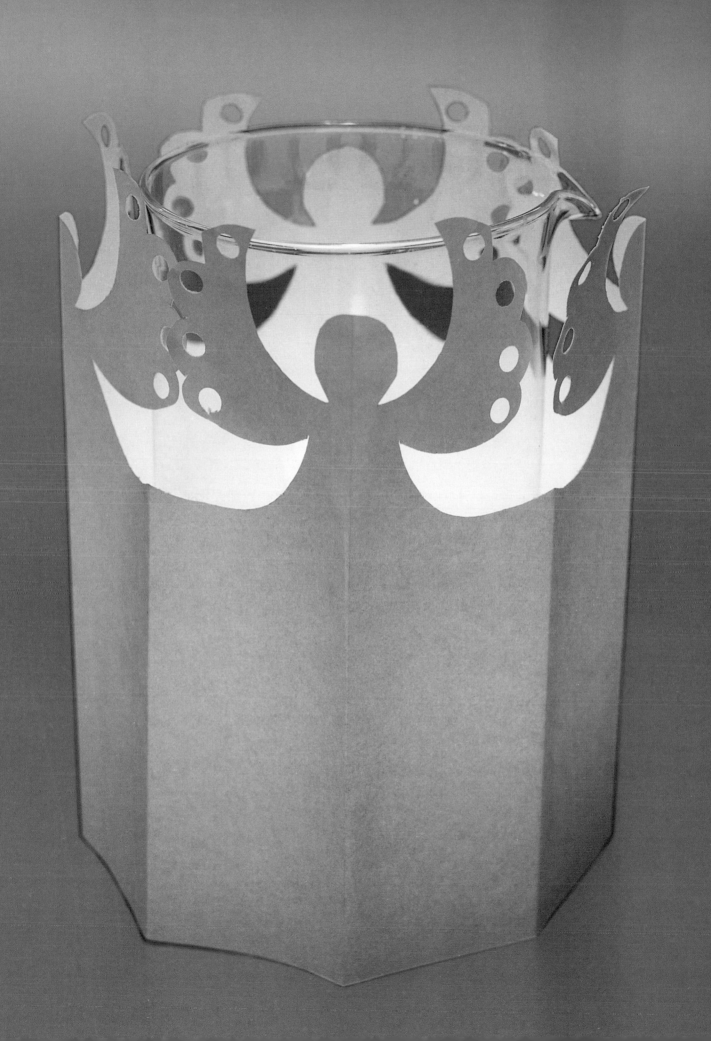

Quilling TECHNIQUES

Quilling, sometimes called paper filigree, is the centuries-old art of creating decorative shapes from narrow strips of paper. Various shapes can be formed, usually by first rolling the strips into tight coils, then allowing them to unroll slightly and pinching them. These can then be combined to make patterns, using the various shapes and colours to good effect. No special tools are needed – you can roll the strips around a cocktail stick – though quilling tools and pre-cut paper strips are readily available from craft suppliers.

Cutting paper strips

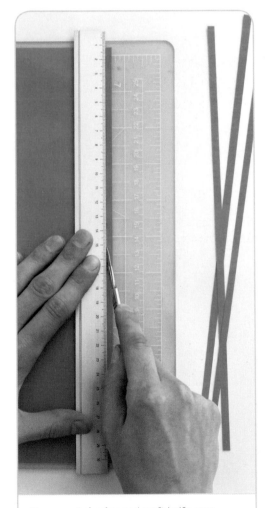

Use a metal ruler and craft knife over a cutting mat to cut narrow strips from a sheet of coloured paper. Strips can be any width, though 3mm (⅛in) is the most popular size.

Basic quilling

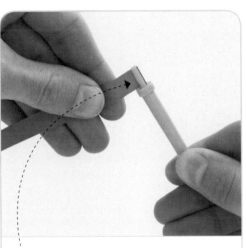

1 Insert one end of a paper strip into the slit in the quilling tool (or wrap the end around a cocktail stick).

2 Twirl the tool with one hand while guiding the paper strip with the other, to wind the paper into a tight coil.

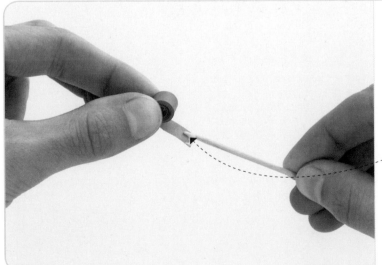

3 Slip the paper coil off the tool. If you want to use the quilled strip as a tight coil, use a cocktail stick to dab a spot of PVA glue to the end of the strip and stick in place.

Creating shapes

1 Allow the coiled paper to relax slightly to make a round coil that is more open in appearance, then glue the end in place.

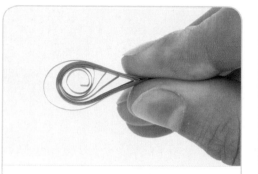

2 To create a teardrop shape – useful for flower petals and leaves – allow the coiled paper to unwind slightly before glueing the end in place, then pinch the coil in one place between finger and thumb.

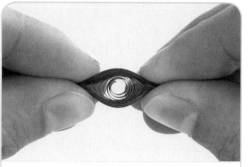

3 To create a shape reminiscent of an eye – known as a marquise – allow the coiled paper to relax slightly, glue the end, then pinch the coil in two places, as shown.

4 For a triangular shape, pinch a coil that has relaxed slightly in three places. This shape is useful for flower motifs and leaves.

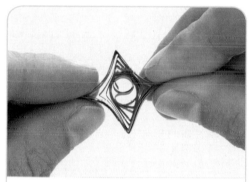

5 A relaxed coil pinched in four places is known as a star.

6 Create this heart shape by rolling a paper strip from both ends, then crease the centre of the strip so that the coils face each other.

Glueing and arranging

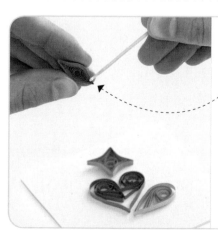

1 Use small dabs of PVA glue – which becomes transparent once dry – to glue shapes to a background.

2 Combine various shapes to make motifs that can be used to decorate greetings cards, labels, pictures, and book covers.

Quilled paper picture PROJECT

You will need only the most basic materials – strips of coloured paper, a quilling tool or cocktail stick, a piece of backing card, and glue – to create a decorative quilled picture. To display your work of art, choose a fairly deep frame, or mount the picture using a deep mount that accommodates the thickness of the paper strips and prevents them from touching the glass.

YOU WILL NEED

- 3mm (⅛in) wide paper strips in blue, yellow, red, green, and pale green
- quilling tool
- PVA glue
- cocktail sticks
- 25 x 20cm (10 x 8in) backing card

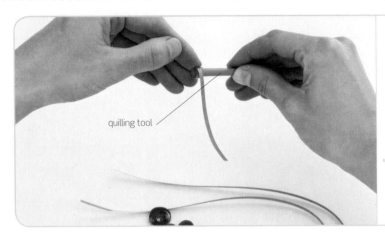

quilling tool

1 Make 15 coils in blue: make three tight coils, eight a little more relaxed, and four more relaxed still. Glue the ends in place.

2 Make three tight coils in yellow, then make seven teardrop shapes in red for the petals, glueing the ends in place.

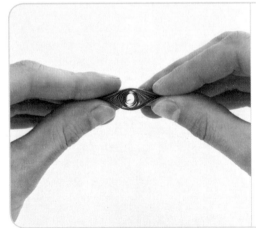

3 Make six leaves using green paper strips and glue the ends.

4 Fold pale green strips in half lengthways to create stems. Apply glue sparingly along the edges of the paper and place on the backing card, using the final image as a guide. Glue one yellow coil to form a flower centre.

5 Arrange the other quilled shapes in position. When you are happy with the arrangement, glue each shape in place.

Card-making TECHNIQUES

Homemade greetings cards are fun to make and show the recipient that you really care. Traditionally sent on special occasions such as birthdays and Christmas, they can also be sent to convey all kinds of messages – such as "thank you" and "good luck", or to convey various sentiments. Best of all, making your own cards requires only the most basic materials and this craft really allows you to express your creativity in a unique and individual way.

Making basic cards

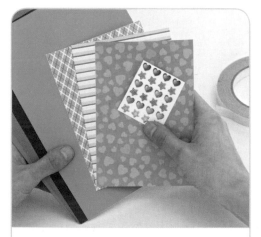

1 There is a wide range of card available to buy, both plain and patterned. For card-making, choose card stock that is sturdy but not too thick.

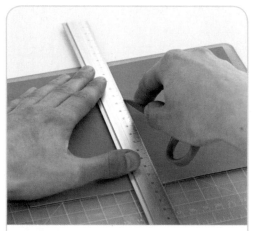

2 A rectangle of card folded in half makes a basic, single-fold card. To make folding easier and neater, score the centre line using the back blade of a pair of scissors and a metal ruler.

3 Cut a piece of paper to the same dimensions as the card or slightly smaller, and fold it in half, for an inner leaf on which to write your message. Punch two holes through both layers, on the centrefold.

4 Thread the ends of a length of ribbon through the holes of both layers and tie with a bow.

5 Additional folds create further design possibilities: a two-fold card gives six surfaces for decoration (three on the front and three on the back). Cut the corners in an interesting shape to add another dimension.

6 This scalloped edge creates an attractive effect. It can be left plain or decorated with stickers.

Making pop-ups

1 Pop-ups add an extra dimension to a single-fold card. Cut two slits at right angles to the folded edge, then score between the ends of these slits, parallel to the edge of the card, to create a rectangular "flap".

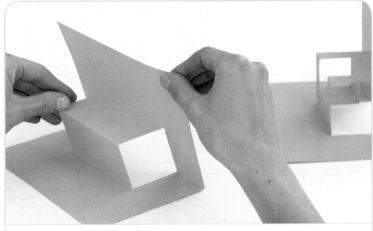

2 Fold across the scored lines to create the pop-up. By cutting and scoring a second set of lines, you can create another level of pop-up. Experiment on scrap paper first to make sure both sets of scored lines work together correctly.

Adding extra decorative elements

1 Combine shapes cut from plain and patterned card scraps to make components to decorate your card.

deckle-edged scissors

2 Use fancy scissors to cut decorative edges. Deckle-edged scissors are available from most craft suppliers, with a wide selection of different blades.

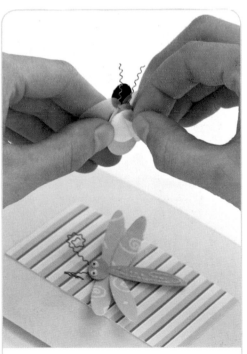

3 To add texture and interest, use small pieces cut from thick card, or use dimensional sticky pads to raise components off the surface of the card, creating a 3D effect.

Pop-up cake card PROJECT

Suitable for a number of different occasions, such as a greetings card or an invitation for a birthday, anniversary, or wedding perhaps – this pop-up card is impressive but uses the simplest techniques to maximum effect. All you need are some colourful card scraps, a steady hand, and a sharp craft knife. Vary the colour scheme to suit your own tastes and the occasion.

YOU WILL NEED

- 2 plain coloured pieces of card measuring 24 x 17cm (9³⁄₄ x 6³⁄₄in)
- metal ruler
- scissors
- pencil
- cutting mat
- craft knife
- printed and white card scraps
- deckle-edged scissors
- double-sided sticky tape
- hole punch
- narrow ribbon
- stickers
- glue stick

1 Score across the centre of one of the cards and fold in half. Measure 5cm (2in) in from each side and make two 5.5cm (2¹⁄₄in) cuts at right angles to the folded edge at each of the marked points. Measure 1.5cm (⁵⁄₈in) in from the cut lines and make two more 3.5cm (1³⁄₈in) cuts.

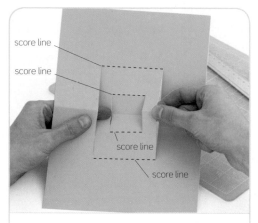

2 Score between the ends of the two pairs of parallel cuts. Open out the card, folding the larger pop-out inwards and the smaller, inner one outwards, as shown.

3 Using striped card, cut a rectangle 10 x 5.75cm (4 x 2¹⁄₂in) for the bottom tier. For the top tier, cut a piece 7 x 4.5cm (2³⁄₄ x 1³⁄₄in) then cut away strips to form candles. For the middle tier, cut a piece 8 x 4.5cm (3¹⁄₄ x 1³⁄₄in) and cut away corners to create a tab to slot into the middle of the inner pop-up.

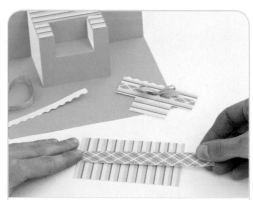

4 From the striped card, cut a piece to cover the top of the pop-up. From contrasting card, cut strips to fit across the tiers. Using deckle-edged scissors, cut strips of white card for borders. Punch pairs of holes in the centres of the card strips, insert short lengths of ribbon, and tie in bows.

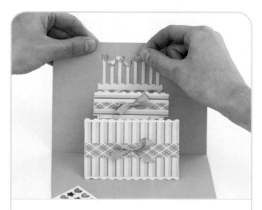

5 Stick the strips onto the tiers using double-sided sticky tape, then stick the tiers to the pop-ups, checking to make sure that the card can still be folded. Decorate the candles and surrounding card with stickers.

6 Score the second piece of card across the centre to make a single-fold card the same size as the first. Apply glue, avoiding the pop-ups, then stick the two cards together to form a neat outer layer.

Skeleton leaf card PROJECT

Dried leaves, spices, and fruit make ideal embellishments for personalized greetings cards. If you want to post any of these home-made, three-dimensional cards, choose those with the least delicate, flattest decorations and cut a piece of card the same size as the card. Cover the front of the decorated card with the card before sealing it in an envelope. This should, hopefully, protect the decorations from disintegrating or breaking in transit.

YOU WILL NEED

- white card
- scissors
- craft knife
- ruler
- bone folder, optional
- found objects such as seedheads, twigs, and leaves in different sizes, dried flat
- spices such as star anise and cinnamon sticks
- dried ingredients such as orange slices and bay leaves (optional)
- PVA glue

1 Cut a piece of card to your desired size. Score lightly down the middle of the card in a straight line using the back of a craft knife and a ruler. Press lightly as you do not want to cut through the card.

2 Fold the card in half along the scored line. Use your fingertips to form a neat crease, or use a bone folder (available from good craft shops and online stores).

3 Stick a dried leaf onto the front of the card using small dabs of glue. The reason you do not brush glue all over the entire leaf is because, in its delicate state, the skeleton will disintegrate if it becomes too wet.

4 Stick two smaller leaves on top of the larger leaf. Fan them out slightly so that they overlap each other but are not on top of each other. Attach one star anise at the base of the leaves. Set aside until the glue is dry.

Fabric Christmas card PROJECT

This attractive card can be easily adapted: use a loop of ribbon instead of string, or punch two small holes close together near the top of the card, thread through wool or twine, and tie it in a bow; or cut out and sew together two fabric shapes and fill the centre with sweet-smelling dried lavender. Don't cut the shapes too small, or you may find them fiddly to sew and turn inside out.

YOU WILL NEED

- pencil
- scrap of white card
- scissors
- scraps of fabric with an interesting pattern and texture
- string
- button or bead
- PVA glue
- craft knife
- ruler
- rectangle of white card

1 Draw a boot shape, or outline of your choice, onto a piece of thin white card. Cut neatly around the outline with a pair of sharp scissors to create a template. Place the template onto a piece of fabric and neatly cut around it.

2 Thread a short length of string through two holes in a button or bead and secure the ends in a small knot on the underside. The string will then form a loop.

3 Glue the knotted end of the string loop to the back of the fabric shape. Position the loop so that it emerges from the centre of the boot and the knot sits just below the top of the boot. Set aside until the glue is dry.

4 Lightly score down the centre of the rectangle of white card – the size and exact shape is up to you. Use the back of a craft knife and a ruler to make a crease but do not cut right through. Fold the card in two and glue the boot on the front.

3D card PROJECT

The next time someone you know has a birthday, or is celebrating an anniversary, instead of buying them a card from a store, why not make your own? You can personalize the card to make it look exactly how you want and the recipient will really appreciate the effort you've made. Try a selection of paper-weaving and origami designs as shown here.

YOU WILL NEED

- pencil
- 1 sheet of yellow paper
- scissors
- 1 small sheet of pink paper
- 1 large sheet of pink paper
- glue stick or PVA glue

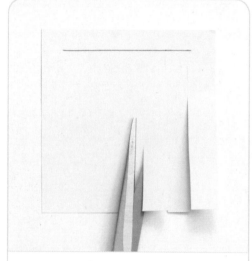

1 Draw a faint pencil line, 2.5cm (1in) away from the top of the yellow paper. Cut strips every 2.5cm (1in) along the bottom of the paper, towards the line.

2 Cut 2.5cm (1in) wide strips out of the pink paper. Thread the pink strips of paper over and under the strips of yellow, making a weave.

3 Repeat this process until you have created a chequered pattern. Secure the flaps at the edge of the design with small dots of glue.

4 Fold the larger piece of pink paper in half twice and then open it out again. Cut out a shape, such as a heart, in the bottom right-hand corner.

5 Glue your chequered pattern to the opposite side from your cut-out shape. This will result in the woven paper showing through the aperture.

6 Refold the pink paper to form a card.
Draw on additional details if you wish.
Write your message inside.

Party invitations PROJECT

Birthday party and baby shower invitations, as well as announcements and celebratory cards always look more heart-felt when handmade, and what better media than paper to make and decorate your invitation. By adding a few embellishments and cutting out a few paper motifs, your design will look great, and everybody will be impressed by your creativity

YOU WILL NEED

- white card
- pink card
- pencil
- ruler
- scissors or craft knife
- glue stick or PVA glue
- coloured plain and patterned paper
- selection of felt shapes, sequins, ribbons, and glitter
- envelope
- double-sided sticky tape

1 Fold the white card in half to form a card blank. Cut the pink card to the size of one half of the card blank. Draw a 2.5cm (1in) border around the pink card and cut around it to create an aperture.

2 Attach the frame to the front of the white card with glue. While the glue is drying, cut out the balloon and gift-box shapes from the coloured paper. Accessorize the shapes with ribbon and sparkly jewels.

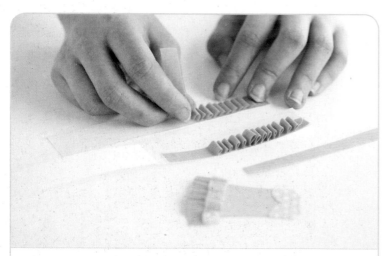

3 Cut out a card dress shape. Use glitter paper for the coat hanger. Fold fabric strips and stick to the dress with double-sided sticky tape as ruffles, see **concertina folding** on p.42.

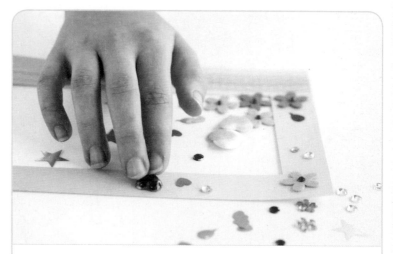

4 Decorate the frame with embellishments. Glue your balloons, dress, and gift-box decorations to the white card inside the aperture. Add a thin line of glue from each balloon and sprinkle with glitter.

5 Wrap a length of ribbon around the envelope, and glue on more sequins. Write inside the card.

Box-making TECHNIQUES

Box-making is also known by the French term "cartonnage" and covers a variety of techniques. In its simplest form, this craft consists of cutting a form from flat card using a template, cutting out the shape, scoring and folding, then assembling it into a box. Gift boxes are readily available from stationers and craft shops but it's much more fun – and cheaper – to make your own.

Choosing materials

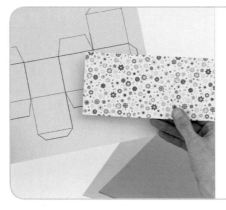

Choose your materials carefully. For a small box, thin card will do, but for a bigger box, the card needs to be slightly thicker. Photocopy the template on p.93 onto the wrong side of the card, enlarging it to the desired size, or copy then trace it onto the card.

Cutting

1 Place the card on a cutting mat and cut out the outline of the box using a craft knife and metal ruler. Take care not to cut along the internal fold lines.

2 If you prefer, you can use scissors to cut out the outline.

Scoring

1 For a neater finish, score along the fold lines before folding them. Make sure the drawn lines are on the inside of the box and, using a metal ruler as a guide, run the blunt edge of a craft knife blade over the fold lines.

2 Once you have scored all the fold lines, fold inwards along each one.

3 For really crisp fold lines, run along the folds with a smooth instrument, such as the back of a spoon. The proper tool for this job is a bone folder, so use this if you have one.

Making labels

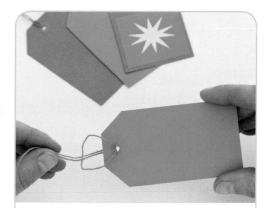

Use card offcuts to make labels. Cut small rectangles of card then trim off two corners. Apply a round sticker and punch a hole in the centre of the sticker. Add a loop of cord. Leave plain or decorate with a paper cutout.

Making decorative bows

1 To make a bow, cut two strips of crepe paper with the grain running widthways. Use one strip for the loops and one for the tails, cutting the ends in a V-shape. Place the loop in the centre of the tails.

2 Cut a third strip and fold in each long edge to the centre. Wrap this piece twice around the centre of the bow, then cut off excess and glue or tape the cut end to the underside of the bow.

Making paper flower decorations

1 Make a paper flower centre by wrapping two or three layers of tissue paper around a ball of wadding. Using fine wire, bind the ball to one end of a length of thick paper-covered wire.

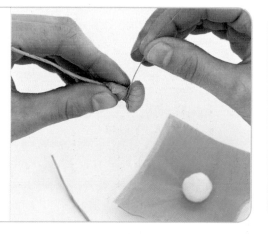

2 Cut petals from crepe paper with the grain running lengthways down each. Flute the edges then gently stretch the centre of each petal to create an attractive curl.

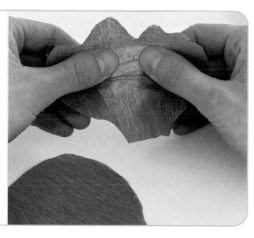

3 Wrap the base of each petal around the flower centre, one at a time, fastening with fine wire. Use a total of about 10 or 12 petals.

4 Conceal the base of the petals by wrapping with a strip of tissue paper backed with double-sided tape. Continue wrapping the strip around the length of the stem to cover it.

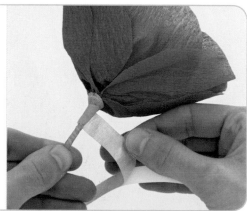

Small gift box PROJECT

This little box is the ideal way to present small, awkwardly shaped gifts. Use the template on p.93 to create as many boxes as you like, in different sizes and using different coloured card. A3 card is widely available in a range of colours and printed patterns. Choose coordinating tissue paper to make paper straw (see p.43) to stuff inside the box.

YOU WILL NEED

- A3 plain or patterned card
- cutting mat
- craft knife
- metal ruler
- scissors
- double-sided sticky tape
- tissue paper, for the paper straw (optional)

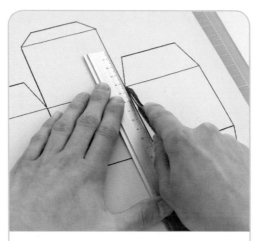

1 Transfer the box template on p.93 to the back of a sheet of A3 card, then score along all internal fold lines using the back of a craft knife blade and a metal ruler.

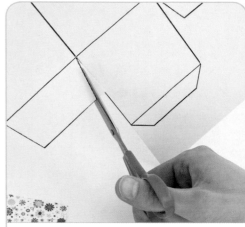

2 Cut out the box using the craft knife or, if you prefer, scissors. Take care not to snip into the internal fold lines.

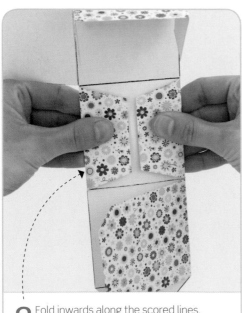

3 Fold inwards along the scored lines, making sure each crease is sharp.

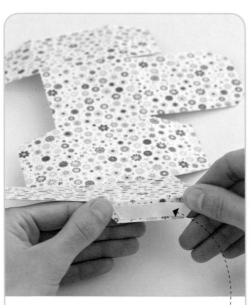

4 Apply a piece of double-sided sticky tape to the right side of the end flap.

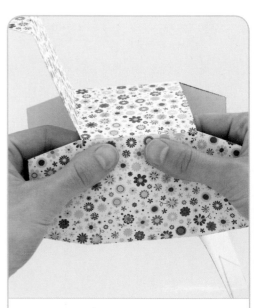

5 Peel off the backing paper from the tape and press the end flap into position to form the four sides of the box.

6 Fold the two pairs of larger flaps inwards. Decide which will be the top and bottom, then stick a strip of double-sided tape to each of the larger flaps on the base and press the square base onto these flaps. Tuck in the smaller side flap, leaving the top open, ready for filling.

Paper and ribbon boxes PROJECT

Opulent wrapping and fabulous packaging can really make a difference when giving gifts. Fill these beautiful boxes with scrumptious treats and give them to somebody to make their day. Alternatively, make a box with a decorative ribbon around the side and a plain lid, then place a paper flower decoration (see p.83) on top.

YOU WILL NEED

- paintbrush
- acrylic paints
- wooden or papier-mâché boxes
- coloured paper or felt
- craft glue, double-sided tape, and glue dots
- glitter and beads
- ribbon and lace
- tissue paper

1 Paint your box sides and lid using acrylic or hobby paints. You can paint the inside if you like but it's not essential. Leave to dry and then brush on a second layer. Cut out a selection of flower shapes.

2 Layer each flower to create a three-dimensional bloom. Secure the layers using glue dots, double-sided tape, or small dabs of glue. Add a bead or sequin. Attach a flower to the lid of your box.

3 Measure the circumference of your box and cut a length of lace, and a length of ribbon, to fit all round. Attach the ribbon and lace using double-sided sticky tape. Repeat steps 1–3 for as many boxes as you wish.

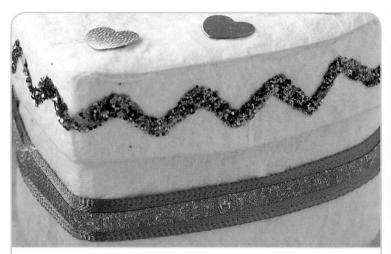

4 Decorate the top of each box with a different design. Here, we have used a zigzag line of glitter glue around the edge. Use small dabs of glue, or double-sided sticky tape cut into small squares to attach sequins or flat-backed gems.

5 For this box top, party confetti is arranged around the edges and secured with glue. Leave until the glue is dry, then line each box with tissue paper and fill with sweets.

Screen printing TECHNIQUES

Screen printing is a fun way to create multiple copies of a simple image. Cut out the stencil from a sheet of thin acetate and place it between the frame and the card on which you're printing, then pull the ink across the screen with the squeegee to print the image.

Preparing the screen

1 Wash the screen by scrubbing it on both sides with a nylon brush and a solution of detergent and warm water. Do not soak. Rinse thoroughly, pat dry with kitchen paper, and leave to dry flat.

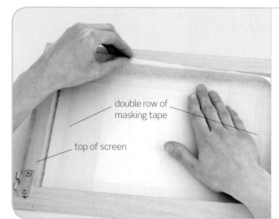

double row of masking tape

top of screen

2 Protect the edges of the screen by taping lengths of masking tape on the front and the underside of the screen. Apply a double row of tape across the top and bottom to create a wider area onto which the inks can be prepared. The unmasked area of the screen is the "canvas".

Preparing the stencils

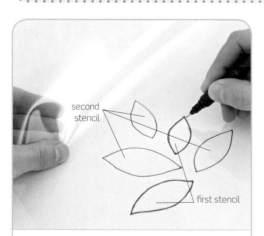

second stencil

first stencil

1 Here we're making a two-colour print, with two red leaves and three yellow leaves, for which we'll need two separate stencils. Using a marker pen, trace the first part of the design (two leaves) on the centre of a sheet of thin acetate. Place another sheet of acetate directly on top of the first sheet and trace the second part of the design (three leaves).

2 Cut out the stencils over a cutting mat using a craft knife. Make sure that the stencils stay flat and do not crease. Always keep your fingers away from the blade.

Registering the print

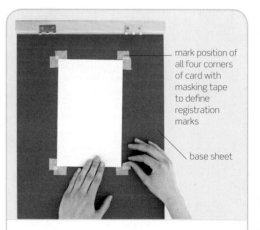

mark position of all four corners of card with masking tape to define registration marks

base sheet

1 Registering ensures that the card and stencil are always in the same relative positions, allowing you to make multiple prints. Place the first blank piece of card on the base sheet and mark the position of all four corners with masking tape. (The card should be smaller than the stencil so that unwanted ink doesn't bleed onto it.)

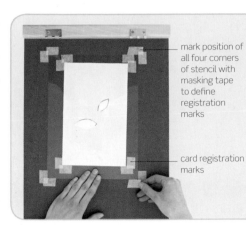

mark position of all four corners of stencil with masking tape to define registration marks

card registration marks

2 Place the first stencil on top of the card so that the design is centred, and mark the position of all four corners of the stencil with masking tape.

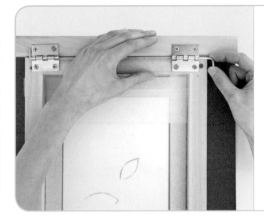

3 Insert the hinge pins to join the screen to the base sheet. Lower the screen onto the card and the stencil, making sure they remain lined up with their registration marks.

Making the first print

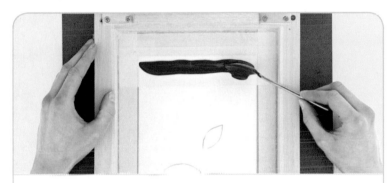

1 Using well-mixed screen printing ink, spoon a line of ink along the width of the masking tape at the top of the screen. Use the squeegee to pull the ink across the screen, angling the top of the squeegee towards you to push the ink through the screen. You may need to do this twice to ensure the ink is pushed through the screen.

2 Use the squeegee to move the leftover ink back to the top of the screen. Lift the screen and remove the printed card. Insert a new blank piece of card and repeat until you have as many copies of the first stencil as you need.

Cleaning up

Before adding the second colour, you must clean the equipment first. Use the squeegee to remove excess paint from the screen, then remove the masking tape. Working quickly so that the paint doesn't dry, use a nylon brush and running water and detergent to wash the screen, squeegee, and stencil. Pat dry with kitchen paper, then allow to dry naturally.

Adding a second colour

Place a previously printed and dried card on the base sheet so that it is lined up with the existing registration marks. Place the second stencil on top of the card so that it too is aligned to its registration marks and the design is centred. Protect the edges of the screen with masking tape, and repeat the printing process, this time using a second colour ink. Repeat until you have a complete set of cards. Clean up your equipment as soon as you have finished.

Screen printed postcards PROJECT

The technique of screen printing is ideal for making multiple printed copies of a design. Here, it is used to make two-colour postcards. You can display the finished postcards in a frame or print the design on a larger piece of card and fold it to make a birthday card for a cat lover.

YOU WILL NEED

- silk screen 90T mesh, 36 x 25cm (14 x 10in) outside measurement
- nylon scrubbing brush
- detergent
- 2.5cm (1in) wide masking tape
- scissors
- 2 sheets of thin acetate
- marker pen
- cutting mat
- craft knife
- 15 x 10cm (6 x 4in) white postcards
- base sheet and hinges
- water-based screen printing inks
- spoon
- 18cm (7in) rubber or plastic squeegee
- kitchen paper

1 Following **preparing the screen** on p.88, wash the screen and leave it to dry flat. Then tape lengths of masking tape first on the front and then on the underside of the screen. Apply a double row of tape across the top and bottom of the screen where the ink will be prepared.

2 Refer to the template on p.92 and prepare two stencils, one for each element of the postcard, following **preparing the stencils** on p.88. Ensure that the two stencils form the whole picture when you hold the sheets together with the edges lined up so that you can use the same registration marks for both stencils.

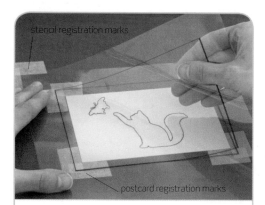

3 Place a postcard on the base sheet and mark the position of all four corners with masking tape. Lay both stencils over the postcard so that the design is centred and mark the corner positions too. Remove the butterfly stencil.

4 Stir the ink, then spoon a line of ink along the width of the masking tape at the top of the screen. Use the squeegee to pull the ink across the stencil, following **making the first print** on p.89.

5 When you have made enough prints using the first stencil, remove the masking tape then wash the screen, squeegee, and stencil in warm soapy water. Pat dry and leave to dry flat.

6 Once the prints have dried, prepare the screen with masking tape again and repeat this process using the second stencil to add the second colour.

Templates

Stationery stamp (pp.40–41)

Postcard (pp.90–91)

Enlarge by 130% on a photocopier

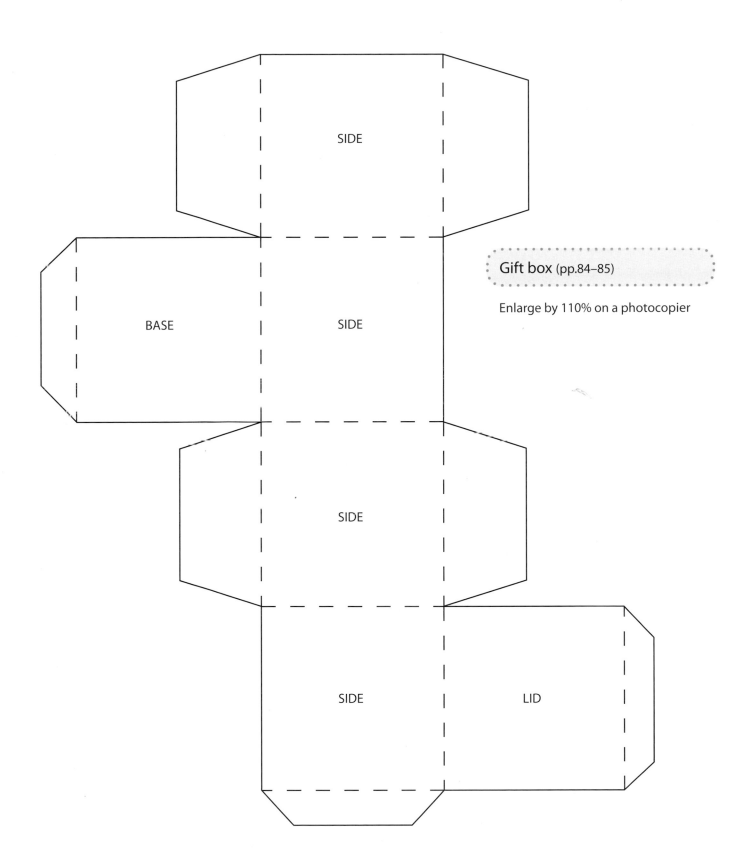

SIDE

BASE

SIDE

Gift box (pp.84–85)

Enlarge by 110% on a photocopier

SIDE

SIDE

LID

Index